Build Your Author Platform in 10 Simple Steps

Find Loyal Followers, Improve Brand Recognition, & Increase Sales With Simple Social Media Marketing Steps & Tips

TRACY J THOMAS

Big Moose Press

NAPLES, IDAHO

Book cover image:
Copyright: alisafovtik/123RF Stock Photo

Visit the link below to get my free newsletter filled with tips and information about social media for writers:

DominatingSocialMedia4Writers.com

ISBN: 069263195X
ISBN-13: 978-0692631959

DEDICATION

This book is dedicated to all the writers who have dared to dream of seeing their words in print. May you continue to pursue the passions of your soul and believe in your gifts enough to share them with the world

Table of Contents

WHY I WROTE THIS BOOK

I wrote this book because I personally understand how difficult it can be for a writer to build their author platform. There are multitudes of ways you can approach the task, and it is easy to feel overwhelmed with the prospect of doing it alone.

I have personally taught many workshops to artists, writers, and organizations on the subject of social media marketing and have written online courses at the University level for creatives that include research and information on how to use social media to their benefit.

If you have the desire to be published by a traditional publishing house you need to build an author platform. If you have already signed a traditional publishing contract, then you know this to be the truth.

The days when traditional publishers handled 100% of the book marketing and sales for their authors has long gone. Today, the majority of publishers expect their authors to play a significant role in marketing their own books. In fact most publishers will not take on an author who does not already have an established author platform.

When it comes to self-publishing, building your platform is imperative to the success of your book. Without a built-in platform at the time you launch a new book, the prospect of your book finding its way towards the top of an already crowded marketplace is very slim.

Building your author platform does not happen instantly. It requires a time commitment and some hard work on your part. I would strongly question anyone who attempts to sell you information that claims to be some "top secret formula" for garnering tens-of-thousands of followers and six-figure book sales overnight.

If by a very slim chance you do find one that works, I would bet my bottom dollar it requires an additional large investment of your money and an even larger amount of your time to implement this supposed "top secret formula."

There is no magic pill, for that I am sorry. But there are definitely many invaluable tools available to help you build your author platform in a manner that is flexible enough to fit into your schedule and for the most part free.

When you have a roadmap in hand to follow, the task will not seem as daunting. My goal is to offer up the beginnings of this roadmap in this book and provide you with additional support and information through my newsletter, upcoming books, and courses.

WHY YOU SHOULD READ THIS BOOK

This book will help you reach beyond your current fold of family, friends, and devoted followers, and provide you with the information you need to find more targeted connections on social media.

In this guide, I provide you with 10 action steps to help you build your author platform. Each action step includes from two to eight proven tips to help you successfully implement each action consistently over time.

There are no magic formulas that will build your platform overnight, so please ignore those people who attempt to entice you to pay big dollars to receive some top-secret formula or a ton of instant followers. If it were real, everyone would be doing it.

The tips in this book are time-tested actions that will help you build a following of targeted, loyal individuals that will make a difference in your visibility and ultimately in your book sales.

If you make the commitment to do at least one tip described under one action step every day in this book, you will begin to see your platform grow exponentially.

Chapter 1. So What Is An Author Platform?

Honestly? The term "Author Platform" is just another catch phrase or buzzword created and used by the people in the book industry to talk about an author's social media and web presence, level of fan engagement, the size of their current readership, and the types of connections they have built with bloggers, agents, publishers, and other authors in their lives.

In other words, your author platform is basically the number of people you can broadcast information to about yourself or your writing at any point in time. It is also about the level of influence you have over them in regards to their willingness to help you get your message out to others.

Publishers won't usually take a gamble on you unless you can show them you have some credible relationships, rapport, and engagement with a built-in audience to whom you can market your books.

Traditional publishers have differing views as to the number of followers an author should have before taking a chance on working with them. Since it varies widely, it is best to focus 100% on your percentage of growth and not on the amount of followers you have at any given moment. It is a lot more reasonable and viable to present a publisher with the percentage of growth of your following by using data from analytical tools on your social media sites. That will provide them with an indication of how devoted you are to building your platform over time.

Your total number of followers can be fleeting, due to a few seedy marketers who are trying to pick up false numbers by following the masses. Those individuals usually un-follow the moment they realize you are not going be enticed to follow them back.

The true proof of your author platform lies in the number of individuals on your social media sites who actually stick around, engage with your posts, and have a focused interest in what you have to offer.

As a self publisher, analyzing your data and watching your percentage of growth in all channels and gauging user engagement, will help you to make adjustments to your efforts and the types of posts you put out there based on what appears to appeal to your user base.

When it comes to self publishing, chances are slim your next great American novel will be discovered overnight and become a success on its own without a strong core of people who are already following you when you begin your concerted marketing efforts.

According to Bowker, in 2013 there were in excess of 450,000 self-published books alone. That number does not account for the number of books in the market published by way of the traditional route. That is a whole lot of competition.

Although this does create a somewhat grim picture of the saturated and competitive marketplace for books, and the investment of time and effort it takes to get one noticed, I did not write this book for the purpose of dissuading you from being an author. On the contrary, I wrote it to encourage and to help you build your platform the right way, so it becomes easier to market and sell your books over time, or to land that traditional publishing contract you may desire.

Countless numbers of individuals have experienced success by building a strong following on social media that provided them with a built-in audience that they market to whenever they release new work. The key is to build a platform of individuals who believe in you as a writer and as an individual, and who are interested in the subjects you choose to write about.

It is also important to note that the primary focus of social media should be in building relationships and providing your followers with insight to you as an author and human being. Your use of social media should focus on building name recognition and leveraging your loyal following's ability to spread your posts to a larger audience.

It should not be used as a daily sales pitch for your books. When you stick to the 80/20 rule of 80% posting of educational or inspirational information and 20% creative pitching of your books, your followers will stick with you and share your posts. They will do this because you have brought value to the social equation and your posts don't feel like an endless stream of spam advertising.

Chapter 2. Why Should I Focus On Social Media Instead of Traditional Marketing Channels?

Back in the year 2,000 there were roughly 738 million Internet users worldwide. That is a lot of people using the Internet! But wait. Just 15 years later there were over 3.2 billion users. That's a 7-fold increase that reflects 43% of the global population in just 15 years! The Internet is not going away and the use of social media is increasing exponentially.

Just stop and think about it for a moment. That statistic means there are over 3.2 billion people from all corners of the globe directly at your fingertips. How exciting is that? Of course I would be foolish to say you could reach them all, but the reality is you now have the capability to get your message out to a significant percentage of those masses through this amazing invention called the Internet by using social media tools for zero or a very minimal cost.

The tables have turned in our favor and the days of forking out big dollars to run traditional print, radio, and television ads to sell more books and garner fans are gone. Think of all the possibilities!

Social media provides authors with an opportunity to enter into conversation with their readers and potential readers. It provides a platform where authors can have ongoing dialogue surrounding responses to their posts. When readers feel they have a personal connection to authors, it is almost a certainty they will continue to purchase the books they release in the future. How often do traditional advertising methods offer such an opportunity for this type of an exchange? Not often.

CHAPTER 3. WHERE DO I BEGIN?

The first step of course is to sign up for social media and blog accounts if you don't already have them. I strongly suggest you create accounts on Facebook, Twitter, and Goodreads at the minimum. Ideally you will create accounts on all of the following:

Facebook (both a personal and an author page) – www.facebook.com
Twitter – www.twitter.com
LinkedIn – www.linkedin.com
Tumblr or Wordpress – www.tumblr.com or www.wordpress.com
Pinterest – www.pinterest.com
Instagram – www.instagram.com
YouTube – www.youtube.com
StumbleUpon – www.stumbleupon.com
Periscope – www.periscope.tv
Goodreads – www.goodreads.com

Since this book is not a how-to on setting up and getting started with each social media tool, if you are new to the game, I suggest you Google instructions for any tool you may have trouble understanding. There are many great online tutorials written on the mechanics for each of these tools.

You can also *DominatingSocialMedia4Writers.com* for my FREE newsletter that will provide you with additional information and tips beyond the scope of this book, plus links to purchase my other affordable how-to guides that cover beginner and advanced users on a variety of topics including social media.

If you lack experience in the use of these tools, I encourage you to sign up first with Facebook and Twitter and start by following the tips in this book for both of these tools. When you begin to feel comfortable with Facebook and Twitter, add one of the other tools on the list each month and apply the tips under the relevant sections of the book.

Now that you are all signed up with your social media accounts, make sure you add all your social media links to your author website or landing page.

What? You have no author website or landing page? This is a very important part of your author platform and should look professional and inviting. Your author website or landing page will provide readers with your relevant contact information and author bio, information about your books, links to purchase them, and links to all your social media accounts.

So, take a deep breath, and jump on into the following action steps. You can follow them in the order they appear, or mix up how you approach them based on the social media tools you have chosen to use.

The one thing I ask you to commit to for now in order to ensure your own success is to focus on a minimum of one action and one tip under that action, each day of the week. Don't overwhelm yourself in the beginning.

For example, on Monday you may decide to choose *Action Step #1: Build Your Twitter Following*. Under this action step, you decide to follow *Twitter Tip #2: Create Your Own Hashtag*. You perform a hashtag search on Twitter and find that the hashtag #TheTitleOfMyBook is not already in use so you create a few tweets and include your new hashtag.

On Tuesday, you make the choice to follow *Twitter Tip #3: Use Hashtag #amwriting*, another tip under this same action you followed on Monday. You create a series of Tweets throughout the day on Twitter that includes the hashtag #amwriting.

And on you go each day until you have circulated through all the action steps and utilized all tips. At that point you would work your way back through from the beginning or pick and choose action steps and tips that you recognize have brought you the strongest response.

So, here we go!

Chapter 4. Action Step #1: Increase Your Twitter Followers

Twitter is a great place to connect with readers, other authors, and people in the publishing industry. It is easy to search and find people to follow in relevant categories and a fun challenge to create short, compelling Tweets that have the potential to be shared by millions. You will find a large amount of fellow authors and readers on Twitter. These people are relatively easy to connect with by using the following tips.

Twitter Tip #1: Enhance Your Twitter Profile
Post author-related information in your Twitter profile including a link to your author website and information on your books. Readers and other authors will have a difficult time finding you if you do not come up in a

search as an author. It will also be easier for them to know more about you and your books if you include a link to your author website or landing page.

In the screenshot below you can see my Twitter banner image includes my book covers and links to relevant sites. My short bio mentions books, photos, nature, artist, social media, and the word "Zen." Each of these words holds relevance to my work and helps my Twitter account to show up in certain searches.

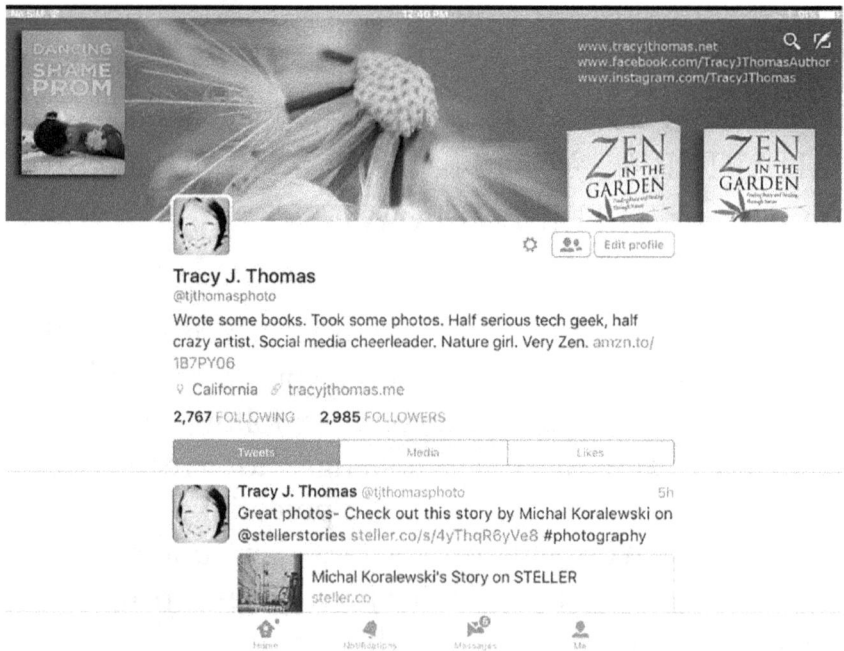

Twitter Tip #2: Create Your Own #Hashtag

Create your own book related #hashtag and use it in relevant tweets. Create several book relevant hashtag ideas such as #ZenInTheGarden (the title of your book) or #ZenAuthor, #ZenBook, etc. (your topic and the word "book" or "author").

Once you have your list of possible hashtags, log onto Twitter and enter your new hashtag into the search box at the top. If you receive no results from the hashtag search, begin using your unique hashtag in Tweets about your book or other relevant subjects.

When you do a search for this hashtag in the future, you will see all the Tweets that have included this hashtag. Encourage your most devoted followers to use your special hashtag when tweeting about you or your book. You can also encourage others to explore your hashtag on Twitter to learn more about your book.

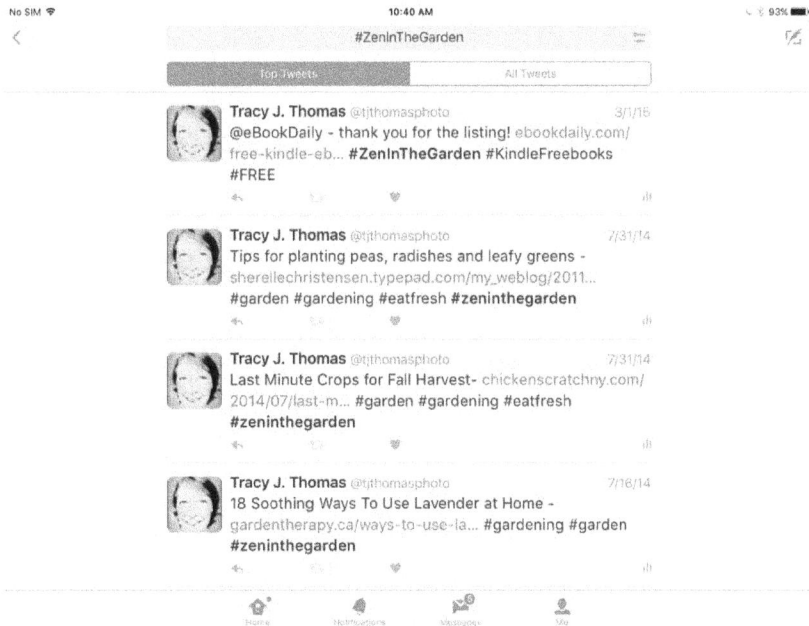

Twitter Tip #3: Use Hashtag #amwriting

Whenever you create a Tweet on Twitter that has to do with writing, your writing process, or your books, include the hashtag #amwriting. If you do a search for this hashtag on Twitter, it will bring up the plethora of fellow writers who also use the hashtag. This will give you a long list of fellow authors to follow. Why follow fellow authors when trying to build your platform? Because authors usually follow back and most love to share posts by other authors knowing theirs will be shared in return. These authors have their own set of built-in readers and followers, so your information will now be in front of more people who can become potential fans of your own books.

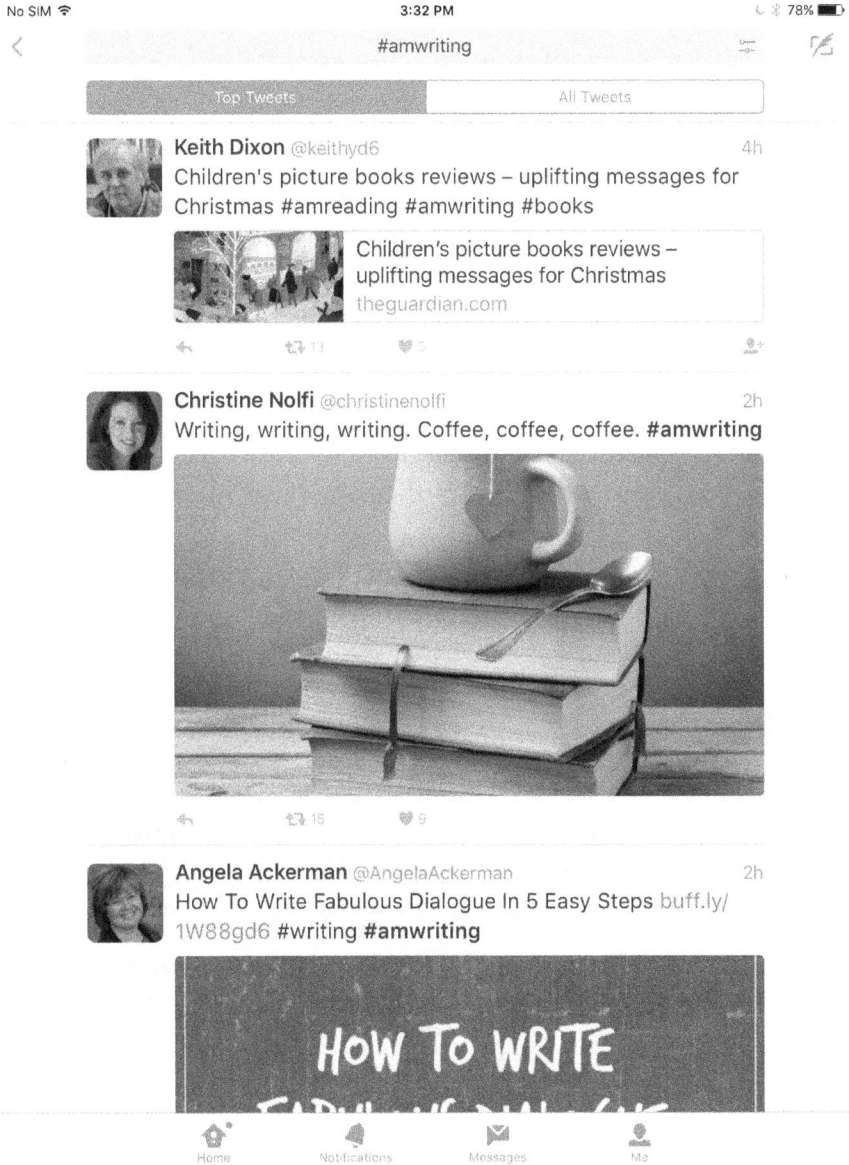

Twitter Tip #4: Retweet, Retweet, And RETWEET

One of the best things you can do on Twitter to gain followers is to retweet interesting tweets made by others. One of the best ways to find tweets to retweet is to enter a hashtag in the search box such as #writing, #fiction, or a hashtag with any other topic of interest related to writing or your specific subject matter. You can also find topics potential readers are tweeting about by entering #amreading in the search box.

Twitter Tip #5: Use Twinitor

There's a great online tool called *Twinitor* that you can use to do a search for the keywords, hashtags, etc. that are used across Twitter. It's a great way to find out who is Tweeting about specific subjects that are tied to your books, interests, etc. You pull your Twitter account into Twinitor and like, retweet, or tweet to other users from within the tool itself. This is an easy way to do a bit of target marketing to users who are already talking about your subject area and who are not already following you on Twitter.

For instance, I used Twinitor to do a search on the keywords "nature," "healing," "gardening," and "peace" so I could connect with users who might be interested in my "Zen in the Garden" book. It provided me with a large return of users and Twitter conversations focused on those specific keywords.

Share the results: ✈ Tweet f Share

🐦 twinitor Add words, phrases, @users and #tags   Search

Right now

Katrina *22 sec ago*
RT @lymecop: Lyme resident agreed £200 for gardening work from jobbing gardeners,and the bill was £350. NEVER use cold-calling tradesmen or...

Liz Carney *24 sec ago*
(Almost) Instant Sacral Chakra Healing Meditation Music - Svadhishthana http://fb.me/3YVa8NAmq

Michael Perry *25 sec ago*
RT @QuibellPaul: Your book-sharing stories: from a grandma's precious gift to an online date gone wrong http://buff.ly/1ZZsnfE

Auntie Can *26 sec ago*
RT
@808s_n_cupcakes: So don't put yourself through that shit bc it will only hinder your healing progress.

BiodiverCité *27 sec ago*
@Zeppoajacky Des crasseux ? Que de mépris envers ces militants qui défendent la nature en péril à laquelle nous devons tous notre existence !

Duko *28 sec ago*
RT @aldubarkadalyn: When the power of love, overcomes the love of power, the world will know peace. - Jimi Hendrix #ALDUB26thWeeksary

savanna *29 sec ago*
RT @MaggieLiedemann: can't wait till I'm 18 so I can date grown boys in peace

Counselling Centre *29 sec ago*
The #Healing Power of #Hugs by @HilaryJHendel in @nytimes #therapy http://goo.gl/07mgJ3

letty *29 sec ago*
RT @TrueChadwick: A mothers love is proof that compassion is our truest nature. @crownofdaisies6 https://t.co/iAs9PtXfxq3

baby squirrel *29 sec ago*
RT @5REDVELVET: [HQ] 151126 RED VELVET at 2015 Ulsan Healing Concert IRENE by @kib_9194 (1) https://t.co/KPYsjNNAZh

216TEMPTATION *30 sec ago*
#: Is My Comfort Zone.... Be So At PEACE

K Brown *30 sec ago*
RT @sharonePack:
★★★★★★★★★★★★★★★★★★★★★★ In #peace I will lie down and #sleep. Lord, you alone keep me #safe. Ps4:8 ★★★★★★★★★★★★★★★

#RIPCJ *30 sec ago*
RT @DJZeeti: world peace a dope idea .. but in reality war is inevitable

Tip: once you enter your keywords or phrase in the search box be patient. It will take a few minutes for Twinitor to retrieve all the results.

www.twinitor.com

Twitter Tip #6: Create Lists

Creating lists on Twitter is an excellent way to organize the people you follow into categories such as readers, authors, publishers, etc. When you place them into appropriate lists their posts won't get lost in your busy Twitter feed. You can make a point of checking in on your different lists daily to read, like, comment, and retweet what you find. The more you engage with your current followers, the more likely others will notice on Twitter and follow you as well.

In order to create a list, choose "Me" to go to your

profile page and click on the gear icon next to the "Edit profile" button. Choose "View Lists" then click the + sign in the top right corner of the screen. Create a name for your list and a description if you want one. You can make your list public or private. If you make your list public, other Twitter users can choose to subscribe to your lists. When you are finished setting up your list, choose "Save." The next screen allows you to do a search for specific followers to add to your list or you can just choose "Done" and add people later.

You can add followers to your individual lists at any time by going to their user profile and choosing the gear icon on the right. From the drop-down list choose "Add/remove from lists," select the appropriate list, and click "Done."

To add one of your followers to a specific list, choose the Add/remove from lists button shown in the screenshot above.

Make sure you check your lists each day and spend some time liking, commenting, and retweeting your followers Tweets.

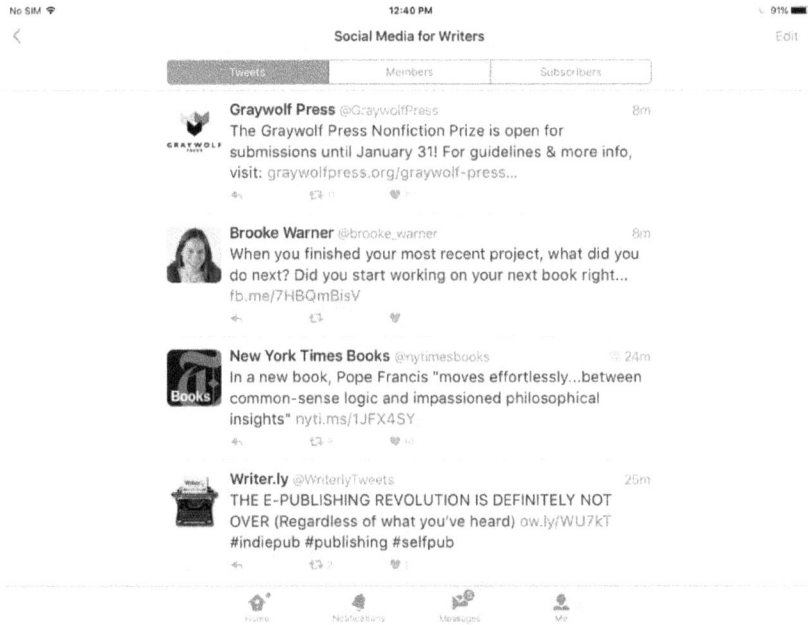

Screenshot from one of my Twitter lists "Social Media for Writers." From this list I am able to check in and like, retweet, and share from the users I assigned to this list.

CHAPTER 5. ACTION STEP #2: INCREASE THE NUMBER OF LIKES ON YOUR FACEBOOK AUTHOR PAGE

Facebook is a lot different than Twitter. It offers a platform where users can interact with followers in a more personal manner compared to the short interface experienced while on Twitter. With a Facebook Author page, you have the opportunity to engage more regularly with your readers and allow them to have a more in-depth glance into the human being behind the words, if you choose.

When someone "likes" your Facebook Author page, it means they become followers of your page and the posts you make will appear in their personal Facebook news feed, where they can share them with their own slew of followers.

Facebook Author pages are accessible to anyone on the

web even if they aren't already a user of Facebook. So, any links back to information on your Facebook Author page out on the web will be accessible to all.

There is much debate surrounding whether or not you should separate your personal Facebook account from your author page. Some say it is best to invite all your readers to follow your personal account since you already have a built-in audience of friends, family, and followers if you have been on Facebook for some time prior to publishing.

My personal feeling is you need to separate the two, primarily for reasons of privacy. An author page's privacy settings should be set to public so anyone can view your posts about your fantastic new book, both on Facebook and across the Internet.

If you make the choice to only use your personal page to market your writing, you run the risk of the rest of the world viewing absolutely everything you post. If you forget to adjust individual post privacy settings this could be embarrassing.

Your loyal friends, family, and followers should jump at the opportunity to like your author page and share it with their friends in order to support your career as a writer.

One of the most important reasons to create a separate author page is the opportunity to run Facebook ads. You cannot run a Facebook ad from a personal account, only from a page.

Facebook Tip #1: Invite Friends to Like Your Author Page

After you have created your compelling author page with your amazing Facebook banner that has images of your books and a link to your author website, reach out to all of your current followers, family, and friends and implore them in your best diplomatic voice, to hop on over and like your author page. Make sure you go back and send out an invite to any new personal account followers every few weeks or so.

Facebook Tip #2: Link Author Page on Your Blog and Website

It seems to be a no-brainer, however, many authors forget to place a link to their Facebook author page on their website or blog. As you build your following on your blog and more outside eyes begin to see your blog posts due to sharing, it is a smart move to have links to all of your social media accounts right there on your blog within clicking distance.

You can use Facebook's page plugin (https://developers.facebook.com/docs/plugins/page-plugin) to create an attractive graphic that can be embedded on your website or blog.

Follow me on Facebook

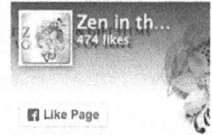

Just a quick post to say thank you all for your support for my recent post about my favorite mobile storytelling app Steller. My Steller story "Pow Wow" has received over 24k page views and yesterday it reached the #2 position of Most Viewed on Steller.

Now let's see if it's possible to double that! https://steller.co/s/5EeDxX32fH6

If you have already had the chance to view "Pow Wow," here is a link to check out my latest, "Timber Men." https://steller.co/s/5FwPcK3KhyH

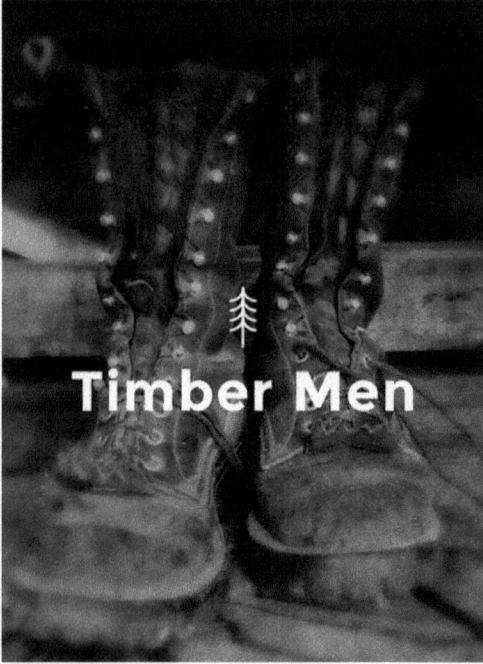

This is a screenshot of three of my Facebook like boxes for specific Facebook pages that appear on my blog. This makes it easier for readers of my blog to find and follow me on Facebook.

Even smarter is to work the link to your Facebook author page into your regular blog posts such as referencing an interesting topic being discussed on your page to your readers. You can mention it somewhere within the blog post content itself, or add it at the end of each post.

Facebook Tip #3: Boost Your Author Page

Part of the beauty of having a separate author page from your personal account is the ability to take advantage of Facebook's advertising and promotion capabilities for very little cost.

When you go to your author page, underneath your banner you will see either "You're almost to xx Likes, promote your page to reach more people" or something similar to "Promote your page for $5."

When you click on this link, it takes you to a section of Facebook where you can set a budget, duration, type of users you want to target, and the keywords to plug in to help you target individuals who use those particular search terms on Facebook. This action will "boost" your page to the newsfeeds of those who you designate in the setup, leading to additional likes.

It is really pretty straightforward and you can limit your total campaign budget to $5 or more depending on your personal marketing budget.

No SIM 📶	2:57 PM	81% 🔋
‹	Promote your Page	Tracy ⌄

👥 **Audience**

Locations
United States ›

Interests
Books, Dogs, Cats, Pets, Life ›

Ages
18 ——————————————————————— 65+

Genders

All	Men	Women

Ⓢ **Daily Budget**

◉ $5 — Est. Likes: 5 - 21

○ $10 — Est. Likes: 10 - 41

○ $15 — Est. Likes: 15 - 62

○ $20 — Est. Likes: 21 - 82

○ Choose Your Own

📅 **Schedule**

○ Run this ad continuously

◉ Choose when this ad will end

○ 7 days — Ends Jan 19, 2016

○ 14 days — Ends Jan 26, 2016

○ 28 days — Ends Feb 9, 2016

◉ Run this ad until — Jan 22, 2016

Promote Page

By tapping the above button you agree to Facebook's Terms and Advertising Guidelines.

This is a screenshot of the promotion setup page on Facebook. You can choose to set your targets for age, interests, and location as well as your daily budget and schedule.

You can also monitor the effectiveness of your boosts during and after each campaign in order to judge their effectiveness.

Facebook Tip #4: Like and Engage With Other Pages in Your Niche

Do a search for Facebook pages of other authors, book clubs, publishers, or topics related to your interests, focus, or expertise and like them from your Facebook author page.

Take the time to like and reply to their posts in an engaging manner but make sure you are doing so as your Facebook author page and not your personal account. Doing so will draw attention to your own author page and will most likely result in additional likes on your page.

Facebook Tip #5: Add Facebook Page Link in Blog Comments

When you post insightful, relevant comments on popular blogs, use your Facebook author page link when they ask for the URL in the comment box.

CHAPTER 6. ACTION STEP #3: INCREASE THE NUMBER OF PROFESSIONAL CONNECTIONS ON LINKEDIN

LinkedIn is considered the epitome of professional networking sites that provides its users with a certain level of credibility. Over the years it has morphed from a "strictly business" model into a platform that offers functionality akin to other social media tools such as Facebook.

The nice blend of professional and social creates the perfect environment for authors to get their work in front of the movers and shakers in the industry, and provides them with an opportunity to make important and relevant connections as well as fans.

LinkedIn Tip #1: Join Relevant Groups

LinkedIn should be treated like any other social media platform - it's not a place to "sell" but it is a place to "market." You can start to build connections by joining groups that are focused on your particular interest in writing or simply fall under the larger umbrella such as "authors, writers, publishers, etc." To find groups to join, just hover your mouse over "Interests" in the menu at the top and choose "Groups." You can then click on "Discover" and browse through a list of suggested groups or enter a search term such as "authors" in the general search box at the top then choose "Groups" from the left menu. Read through and find the groups that interest you and click "join." The attached example shows a partial list of the 1,343 results that showed up when I entered the search term "authors."

LinkedIn Tip #2: Enhance SEO

Enhance your SEO (Search Engine Optimization) within LinkedIn and on the web by adding keywords to the website links within your LinkedIn profile. Just click on "Contact Info" in your profile then under "Websites" at the bottom, click on the edit button next to the listing of your websites and choose the "Other" category next to your "websites" instead of "Personal Website" or

"Blog." This will open up an additional text box where you can write descriptive keyword titles next to the URL of your website, blog and Facebook author page. Try to use key words similar to the ones used in your header and titles.

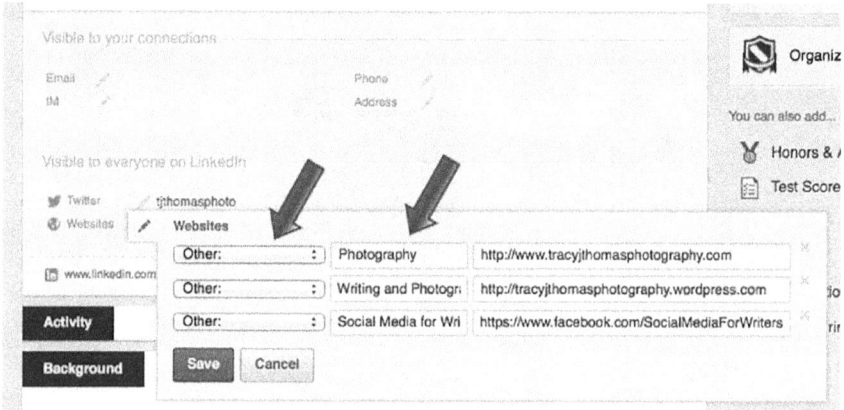

LinkedIn Tip #3: Optimize Your Profile for Search
Optimize your personal profile on LinkedIn so you will rank higher in a general search by using keywords and phrases in your heading and title such as "author," "novelist," "freelance writer."

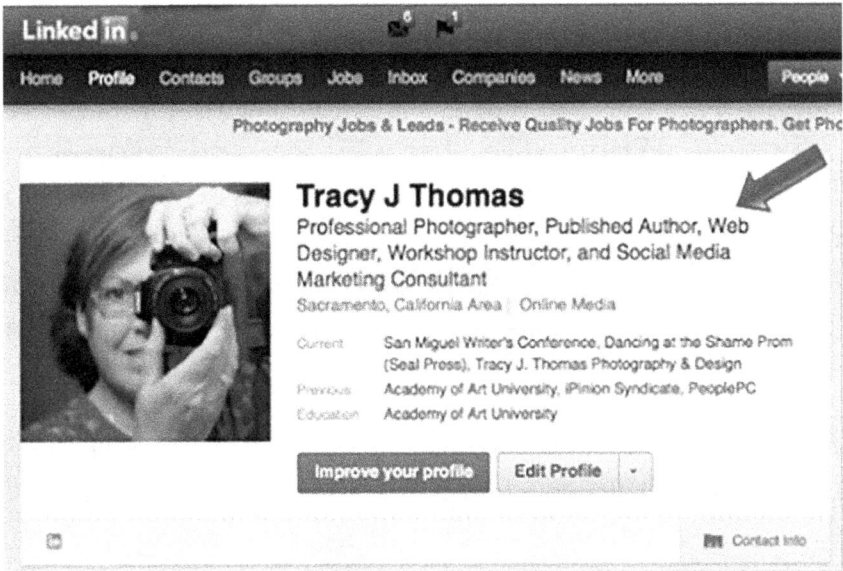

LinkedIn Tip #4: Make Regular Updates

Another great way to make new connections is by publishing posts directly on LinkedIn, sharing links to your blog posts, or posting relevant photos. Make sure you set your privacy settings so that all your posts can be seen in the general newsfeed and not only by your current connections.

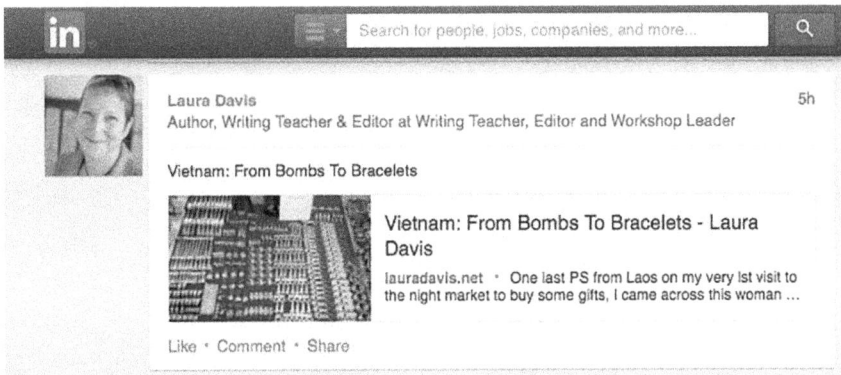

The above image is a screenshot of a post on LinkedIn created by author Laura Davis that appeared on the news feed. Note the words "Author, Writing Teacher & Editor at Writing Teacher, Editor and Workshop Leader." These are all keyword terms she used to describe herself and her services on her profile page. Whenever she posts a LinkedIn update, these terms appear on her post as well as in Google and LinkedIn searches.

LinkedIn Tip #5: Add a Book Excerpt or Other Media

One of the least used features on LinkedIn is the ability to visually enhance your profile by adding photos, slideshows, videos, or documents. If you have an excerpt from your book, upload the PDF file to your profile page.

To do this, go to your profile page and scroll down below the "Add a section to your profile" area. You should then see all your current sections such as "Summary," "Experience," etc. At the bottom of each section you will see "Add Media" with icons for adding documents, photos, links, videos, or presentations. I suggest you add your book excerpt PDF to your "Experience" section under any of your Author entries for the relevant book.

Contributing Writer

Dancing at the Shame Prom (Seal Press)

April 2012 – 2012 (less than a year)

Contributing writer to the Seal Press anthology "Dancing at the Shame Prom: Sharing the stories that kept us small" (Sep. 2012).

Add Location

Add Media: 📄 Document   📷 Photo   🔗 Link   ▶ Video   🎪 Presentation

Add to Position: Contributing Writer at Dancing at the Shame Prom (Seal Press)

http://   or   **Upload a file**

Supported Providers

Continue   Cancel

The above screenshot shows a portion of my "Experience" section on LinkedIn. Near the bottom you will see "Add Media." When you click on "Document" next to "Add Media," you will be able to upload your book excerpt PDF from your computer there.

Click on the document icon and choose either a link to your document on the Internet, or the PDF file you want to upload from your computer. Make sure the file you are uploading is 15mb or less.

You might also think about adding your book trailer videos, slideshows of your book covers, links to your book pages or author websites, or any PowerPoint presentations you may have done relating to your work.

CHAPTER 7. ACTION STEP #4: BLOG, BLOG, AND BLOG AGAIN TO GARNER FOLLOWERS AND FANS

I hear far too many authors say, "I don't have time for a blog." My response? A blog will do more for you as a writer than most any other thing you decide to do on the Internet.

If you Google the phrase "should writers have a blog?" you will see a long list of opinions, half stating "yes" and half stating "no." The ironic reality is that the majority of these posts stating an opinion on the subject appeared at the top of the Google search and were links to posts published on *blogs*. Even the "no's." Google crawlers love blogs and will place them higher up in search engine listings on a variety of topics over other sources or publications.

A blog should be one of the cornerstones of your social media strategy for building your author platform. It provides the opportunity to get your writing out there and can serve as a gateway to connect with your audience. They are also the perfect platform for the sharing of information on your books and about you as a writer.

Blog Tip #1: Submit Your Blog to Blog Directories

The above image shows how blog directory logos might appear on the sidebar of your own blog after you submit to them and in turn embed their logo and a link out to their directory. A few of these directories like "BlogTopSites" provide an updating number of the position of your blog in the category in which it resides.

If you have a blog like Tumblr or Wordpress, which I highly recommend you do, you can increase your blog's exposure and improve traffic while building your platform by submitting it to blog directories.

I recommend putting a half an hour aside a few times a week to do a search on Google and then submit to the long list of available blog directories. A lot of them are free in exchange for placing a small .jpg of their logo in the footer or side panel of your blog. Some of them are paid and can gain you additional exposure if you have the money to do so.

Here is a short list to get you started:

Ontoplist.com

Globeofblogs.com

Blogflux.com

Bloglisting.net

Blogdigger.com

Blogarama.com

Blogcatalog.com

BlogTopSites.com

31. **H.I.A.T**

You're looking for some dust, rust, dead objects and buildings, decayed art and such?

Tags: urbex, photo, abandoned, forgotten, decay

Follow

Like it 1

32. **Nikon D90 Blog**

"Nikon D90 DSLR Camera Reviews & How To's. Everything you want to know about the new.. D90 from Nikon"

Tags: d90, books, nikon, tutorials, lenses

Follow

Like it 3

33. **Tracy J. Thomas Photography Blog**

Sharing my love of photography and the inspiration behind my subject matter along with occasional.. tips on HDR photography.

Tags: Fine Art, HDR Photography

Follow

Like it 1

My photography blog has climbed its way up to #33 out of 1,843 photography blog listings on the BlogTopSites directory alone (screenshot above). Check in on your rankings on all directories you submit to and when it begins to rise up the ladder, capture a screenshot to use across your social media accounts to entice others to visit your blog.

Blog Tip #2: Add Social Media Share Buttons

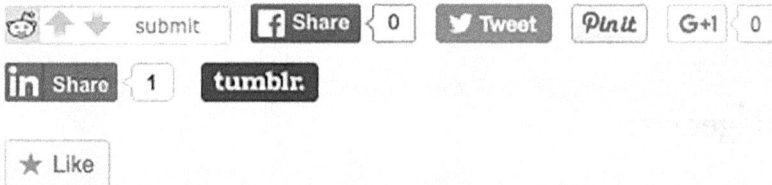

An example of a few of the social media share buttons available as widgets or plugins on most blogs.

Ensure your posts and pages on your blog have social media share buttons. When you have them, your readers will share the blog posts they like with their social media followers and you will begin to receive more traffic, more followers, and more shares.

Blog Tip #3: Write Guest Posts

Contact other authors or people who have blogs in the area of your knowledge or expertise and offer to write a guest post for their blog. The best people to approach are bloggers who already have guest posts listed on their personal blogs. This is a great way to bring attention to your own work, create a network of authors, and gain additional followers to your own blog. In turn, offer other bloggers the opportunity to write a guest post for your own blog.

Screenshot from the MyBlogGuest website.

Another way to find guest blogging gigs is to join MyBlogGuest.com. It is a community of guest bloggers. You can use this site to search for blogs who are looking for guest posts or to find guest bloggers to host on your own blog.

Blog Tip #4: Use Reblog and Like on Tumblr or Wordpress

Use the "Reblog" and "like" features on Tumblr and/or Wordpress in the same way you would use the "like" and "share" buttons on Facebook. When a blog post is reblogged on Tumblr or Wordpress that post will be visible to all followers of the person who does the reblogging. This is a great way to gain new followers. When someone reblogs or likes one of your blogs it is good karma to reblog or like one of their posts in return.

Blog Tip #5: Use Google Alerts

Use Google alerts to find blogs to follow, blog posts to share, and other interesting and relevant topics to blog about.

When you go to google.com/alerts all you do is enter a relevant subject in the search box (a single word or term) and a list of links that touch on those subjects will appear. In order to find blog posts on the relevant subject, simply add the word "blogs" after your relevant term or phrase and Google will bring up a list of blogs with that particular topic. You can then browse through those links to find blogs to follow, posts to share, or information to glean on your topics of interest.

The next step is to enter your email address next to the "Create Alert" button. This will provide you with regular automatic email alerts when new items appear on Google with your chosen relevant search terms. You can choose how often, the sources, the region, etc. under the "show options" button.

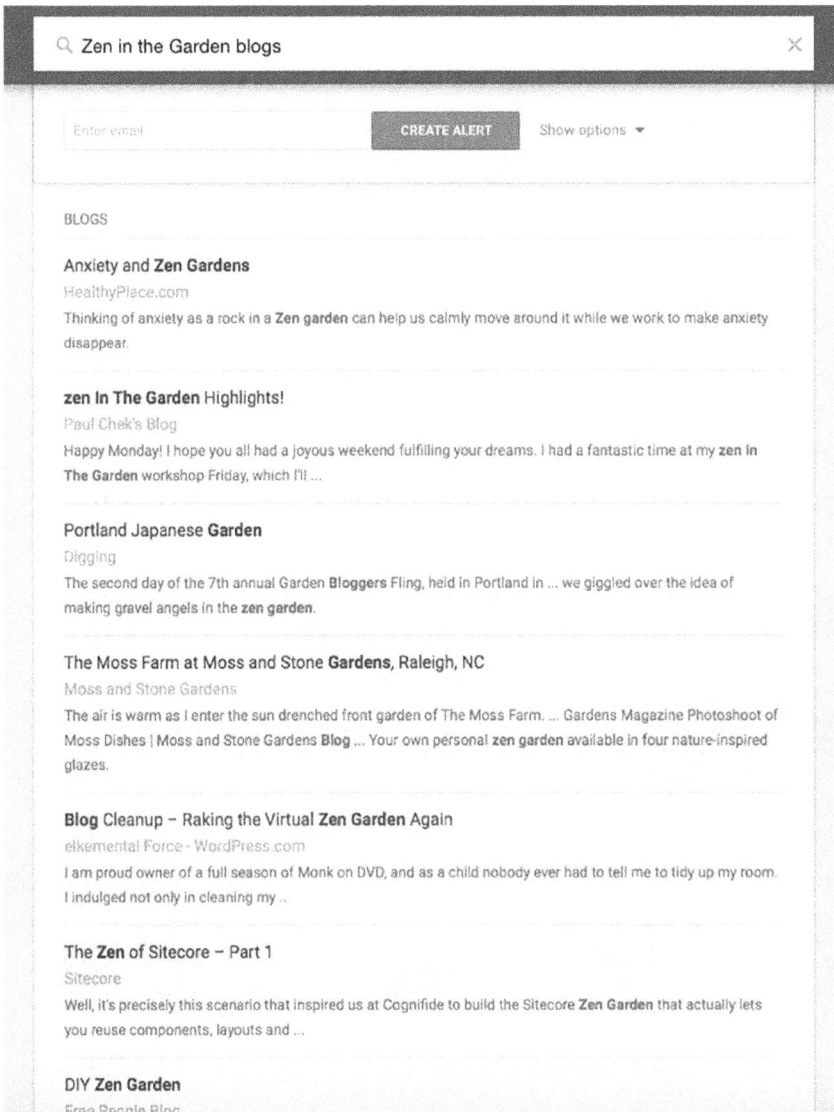

```
Q  Zen in the Garden blogs                                    ×
```

Enter email   **CREATE ALERT**   Show options ▼

BLOGS

Anxiety and Zen Gardens
HealthyPlace.com
Thinking of anxiety as a rock in a **Zen garden** can help us calmly move around it while we work to make anxiety disappear.

zen In The Garden Highlights!
Paul Chek's Blog
Happy Monday! I hope you all had a joyous weekend fulfilling your dreams. I had a fantastic time at my **zen In The Garden** workshop Friday, which I'll ...

Portland Japanese Garden
Digging
The second day of the 7th annual Garden **Bloggers** Fling, held in Portland in ... we giggled over the idea of making gravel angels in the **zen garden**.

The Moss Farm at Moss and Stone Gardens, Raleigh, NC
Moss and Stone Gardens
The air is warm as I enter the sun drenched front garden of The Moss Farm. ... Gardens Magazine Photoshoot of Moss Dishes | Moss and Stone Gardens **Blog** ... Your own personal **zen garden** available in four nature-inspired glazes.

Blog Cleanup – Raking the Virtual Zen Garden Again
elkemental Force - WordPress.com
I am proud owner of a full season of Monk on DVD, and as a child nobody ever had to tell me to tidy up my room. I indulged not only in cleaning my ...

The Zen of Sitecore – Part 1
Sitecore
Well, it's precisely this scenario that inspired us at Cognifide to build the Sitecore **Zen Garden** that actually lets you reuse components, layouts and ...

DIY Zen Garden
Free People Blog

For the Google Alerts search represented in the above image, I entered the title of my book followed by the word "blogs." This brought up a long list of blogs that are posting on topics relevant to Zen or gardening. I was then able to click through each and follow the blogs I felt were relevant.

Blog Tip #5: Author Interviews

Interview other authors who write in your genre, in particular those authors who have a large following, and publish the interviews on your blog. This is another great way to get more eyes pointed towards your own blog.

Additionally, seek out bloggers who interview authors, send them a gratis copy of your book or links to information on your books, and ask them if they would interview you. You can also find several author interview gigs on Fiverr.com starting at a mere $5 per gig.

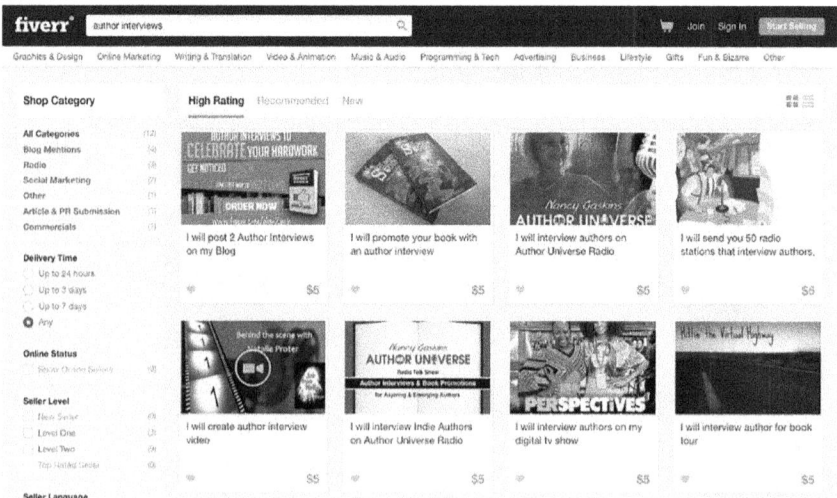

A few of the author interview gigs posted on Fiverr.com

Blog Tip #6: Promote Your Posts

It seems like a no-brainer, but every time you publish a post on your blog, make sure you promote those posts on all your social media channels.

Tracy J. Thomas @tjthomasphoto · 4 Aug 2015
Favorite Mobile Photo Apps - Camera+ for Macro Shots:
wp.me/pQWbM-1r4 via @tjthomasphoto #apps #mobilephotography
#macro

View summary

One of several Tweets I made over the period of a week to drive viewers to one of my blog posts.

When it comes to promoting your posts on Twitter, make sure you Tweet those posts from 5-10 times in a week at different times so all your Twitter followers have a chance to see them.

When it comes to Facebook, make sure you only post them one time each across your personal account and pages. You don't want to look like a spammer.

Blog Tip #7: Add Images of Your Books

Make sure you add images of your book covers to your blog with links out to your book sales page. Place them in the sidebar, on the "About" page, and at the bottom of every blog post you make.

When you add images of your books to obvious places on your blog, every time a pair of new eyes discovers your blog they will see your book covers. Every time you write a new blog, your followers will receive a gentle reminder that you have books available for purchase when they reach the end of your blog post.

A Thousand Words

A picture is worth a thousand words, but words placed together with pictures become the deepest expression of one's soul. – Tracy J. Thomas

Lost in the Woods

By tracyth76

May 15, 2015

- 34,747 Views

Click here:

$2.99

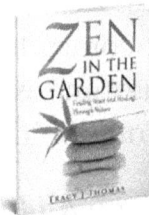

g | Add book

Here is a screenshot of one of my book covers in the sidebar of my blog that links directly to the Kindle version of the book. Viewers see this image every time the read one of my blog posts.

Tracy J Thomas is an award-winning professional photographer, artist, author, and educator located in Northern, California. Her work has been featured in numerous mainstream publications and exhibited in a variety of galleries and private collections around the globe.

She has her M.F.A. in Documentary Photography from the Academy of Art University, San Francisco, and her M.A. from the University of San Francisco.

Tracy was a contributing writer to the 2012 Seal Press anthology, "Dancing at the Shame Prom: Sharing the Stories That Kept Us Small." She also served on Faculty and was a member of the "Women Write Their Lives" speaker's panel at the 2013 San Miguel Writer's Conference in San Miguel de Allende, Mexico.

Her latest book Zen in the Garden: Finding Peace and Healing Through Nature can be prchased on Amazon in both softcover or Kindle editions here.

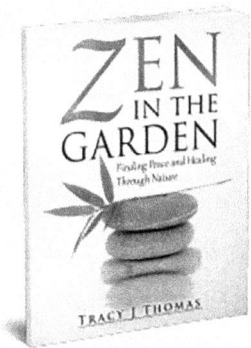

Here is a screenshot of the information section on my "About" page for my blog. I talk about my books in my description, link out to them and include book cover images. My "About" page is one of the most visited pages on my blog so my book receives a large amount of exposure when people visit to learn more about me.

One of the last wonderful things this app offers is the ability to save your images in full resolution. A very important feature when you want to present sharp, professional images.

Overall I would rate this easy to use app as a 4+. It is user-friendly, intuitive, and fun to use!

Oh, and you can purchase the handmade, hemp braided, beaded, Boho Chic, friendship bracelet featured in these photos on my Etsy shop along with much more here! ☺

Click here or on image to purchase your copy today!

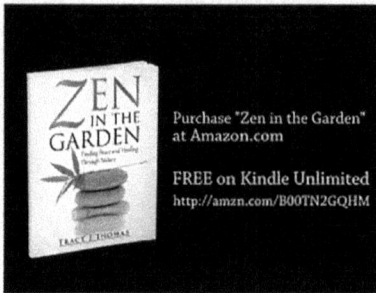

Purchase "Zen in the Garden" at Amazon.com

FREE on Kindle Unlimited
http://amzn.com/B00TN2GQHM

Screenshot of the end of one of my blog posts with a small self-created ad box for my "Zen in the Garden" book.

Every time I create and publish a new blog post I see an increase in my Amazon sales. The beauty of placing these links on your blog, especially a Wordpress blog, is you can measure their effectiveness in your blog sites analytics by gauging the number of clicks you receive to your Amazon page from your book cover links.

The best thing about including your book covers in these places on your blog? It's free advertising! So why wouldn't you take the time to do it?

CHAPTER 8. ACTION STEP #5: BUILD YOUR FOLLOWING ON PINTEREST

Pinterest is a visual tool. People use it for pinning photographs from websites to different boards they create with categories such as "favorite quotes," "pretty jewelry," "my dream home," or "yummy recipes," etcetera.

If you do a search for "books" on Pinterest, you will receive an endless list of pins and boards sporting books from all genres. In fact, if you try to scroll to the bottom of the "books" list under "boards" you will be scrolling for a very long time. What does this mean for you as an author? It means Pinterest users read books! And they read a lot of them.

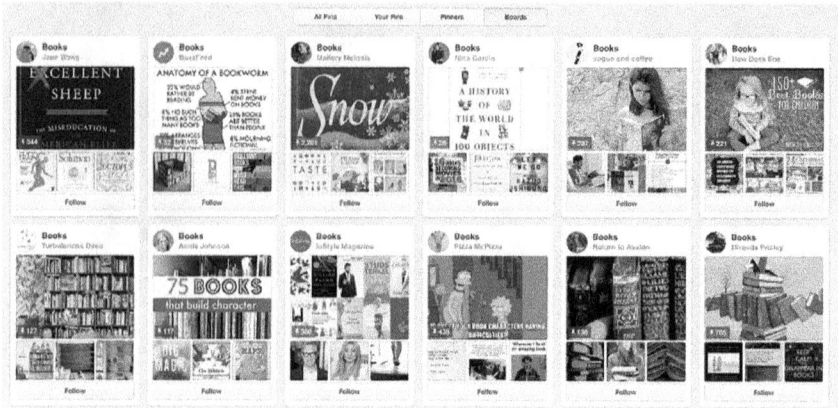

Screenshot of a small portion of the boards created for "books" on Pinterest.

The key to Pinterest however, is to create boards and pins on a variety of subjects in addition to books, in order to draw more people to follow you.

Pinterest Tip #1: Use Quozio to Create Visual Quotes

Users of social media, especially Pinterest, are drawn more often to posts that contain some sort of visual over straight text alone. Quotes are among the most shared text posts on social media. To create a series of visually appealing quotes from your book or manuscript, use the free site Quozio.com. Quozio allows you to choose an attractive layout with various background colors and text (see attached photo). Once you have created several and saved them as jpeg, share them on Pinterest, but also on Twitter, Tumblr, Facebook, and Instagram.

www.quozio.com

"Sometimes when we trust the path we are on, things come up in our journeys that seem to block our progress. These roadblocks are always temporary. When we look at them as nothing more than hurdles to test our passion, then we will find ways over, under, around, or through them. We should use these hurdles as strength and resolve enhancers and not dead ends that destroy our dreams."

Tracy J Thomas from Zen in the Garden

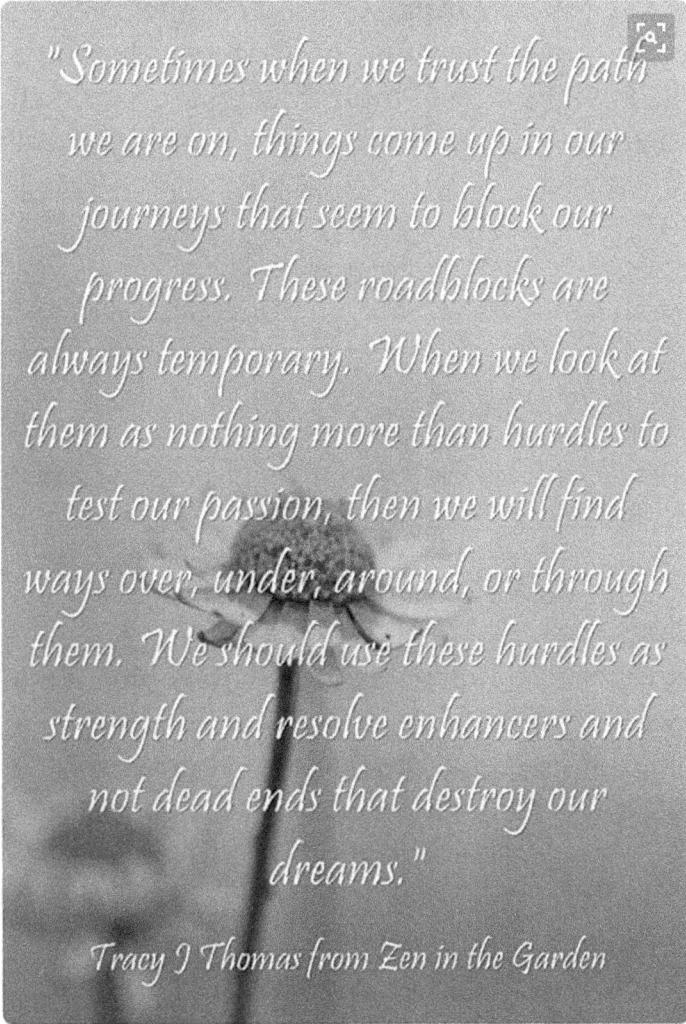

Saved by
Zen In The Garden

Visit

Screenshot of a Quozio created with one of the quotes from my "Zen in the Garden" book that I pinned to my Pinterest.

Pinterest Tip #2: Pin Screenshots of Your Book Reviews

If you have already been published, take screen shots of your positive reviews from Amazon or other places and use them as visuals in posts on Pinterest, but also on Facebook, Twitter, and Tumblr. Make sure you include a link to your Amazon book page or Amazon author page in the posts.

1 of 2 people found the following review helpful

⭐⭐⭐⭐⭐ **The book you MUST read if you're worried that s/he is "just not that into you"**

By Manisha Thakor on December 20, 2011

Format: Hardcover

Lurking inside this delightfully illustrated book is The Secret. If you've ever wondered why that special he or she just seems to be at times on SUCH a different page from you... Marla Press will, in I'M A DOG, YOU'RE A CAT, give you the answer. The subtitle, "love lessons from our furry friends" provides a hint. But I don't want to ruin the surprising insights for you. So let me just say - once you've read this book you will never look at ANY relationship the same way. You will have such clarity - and increased peace of mind - about why we all behave the way we do. Oh, and this book also makes a great gift!

Screenshot of a positive review on Amazon for the book "I'm a Dog, You're a Cat: Love Lessons From our Furry Friends" by author Marla Press that was shared across social media.

Pinterest Tip #3: Pin Inspirational Blogs or Social Media Posts

Sharing inspirational blogs or posts you come across on the Internet into a Pinterest board is a great way to gain additional followers and to promote other writers. You can consider this the "good karma" side of social media. When you share the works and words of others, those people who find your work inspiring will in turn share yours. The attached screenshot is how one writer shares inspirational blog posts of other writers on one of her Pinterest boards.

A sampling of pins by one writer who shares inspirational blog posts on Pinterest.

Pinterest Tip #4: Create a Favorite Quotes Board

Quotes are very popular on Pinterest and are re-pinned often. The Wall Street Journal created a series of images with quotes from their news stories that lead straight back to the story itself through the hyperlink. Think about doing the same by highlighting some of your favorite lines from your own writing that reside on your blog or your website and start a "favorite quotes" board on your Pinterest. Make sure you add a link back to your blog, author page, or Amazon book link. As discussed earlier in this chapter, you can use Quozio to create visuals of your quotes to use for pinning.

Pinterest Tip #5: Use Pinterest Share Button

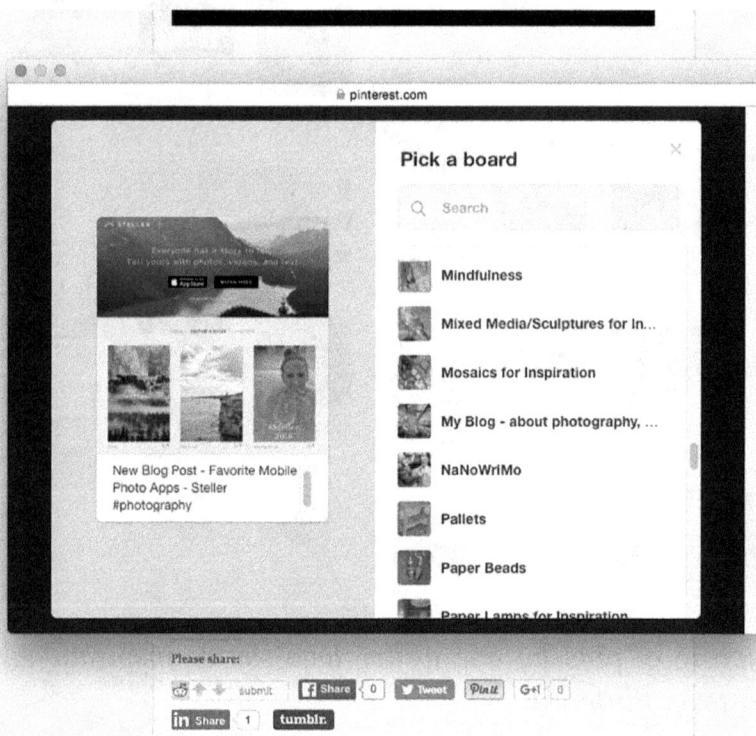

I was able to pin the above blog post directly from my blog to Pinterest by choosing the "Pin it" button. I include images in every one of my blog posts so I can pin each blog post I create.

Create content on your website or blog that can be pinned via a Pinterest share button. For instance, if you write a blog, include catchy visuals like photographs or graphics (make sure you are the one who holds the copyright to those visuals however). That way you can click the Pinterest share button from your own blog or website and pin the images from your posts to a board on your own account that others can later re-pin. These pins will automatically contain the URL from the original post that when clicked, will lead the viewer back to your blog or website.

CHAPTER 9. ACTION STEP #6: INCREASE YOUR FOLLOWERS ON INSTAGRAM

When people think about Instagram, the first thing that comes to mind is photography. The smartphone app was started as a place to share photographs, however over the years smart marketers have learned how to use it to drive people to their websites, blogs, and products.

With over 300 million viewers each month, it stands to reason it would be a smart move to use it in order to market your books.

Instagram Tip #1: Create a Compelling Bio
The amount of words allowed in your Instagram bio are limited, so think up a compelling, creative way to tell them you are an author. Make sure you provide a link to your author website or page.

Instagram Tip #2: Post Photos of Your Everyday Life

Instagram is very visual, so it makes sense to post photographs on the app. Take and share interesting photographs of your writing space. Photograph that stack of books that you have published. Shoot and post photos of you and your dog on a walk by the river searching for inspiration. Post photos of your book readings and book signings. Make a point to share images that allow your followers and potential readers a glimpse into your everyday life.

On the next page is a screenshot that shows a mix of everyday photos and links to my writing that make up a portion of my posts to Instagram.

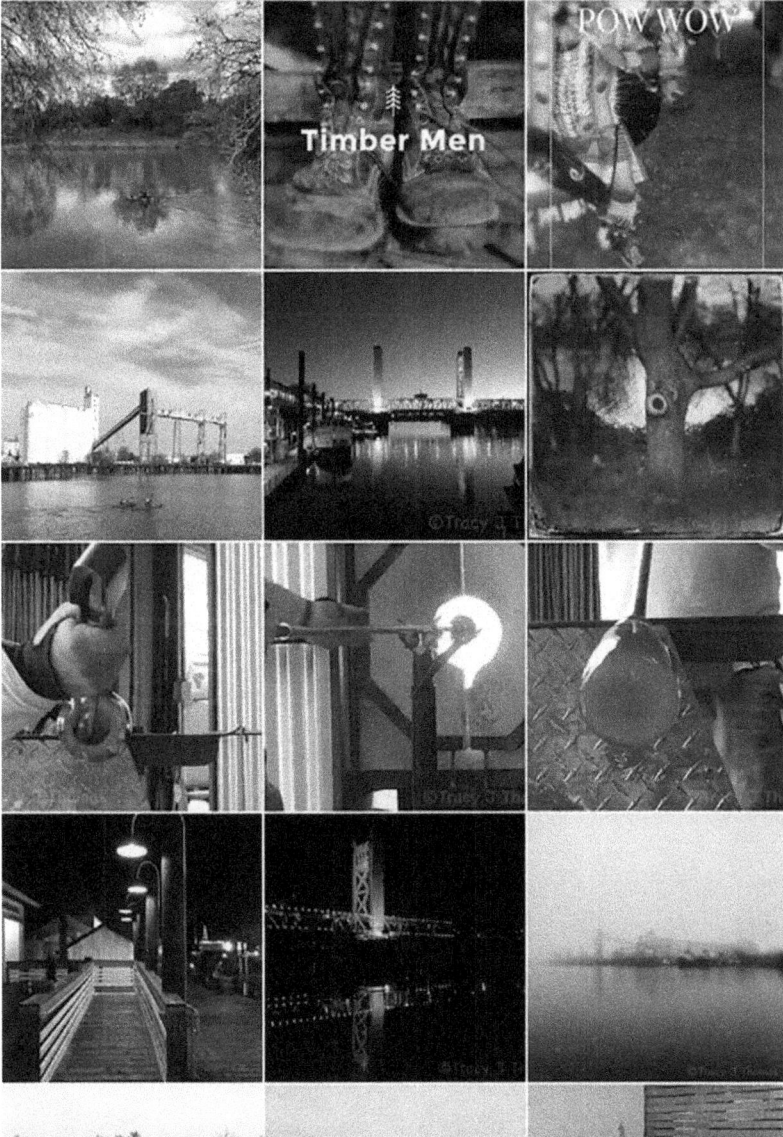

You don't ever have to identify exactly where you are for reasons of privacy; however allowing your followers to see into your life will give them a feeling of being connected to you on a new level.

Instagram Tip #3: Post Short Videos

Instagram also allows users to post short videos. Use your smartphone to capture video of you reading short quotes from your books then post them to Instagram. Record narrated videos of your favorite places to find inspiration. Record a short video of yourself reading positive reviews from your Amazon page. Record your glee when you receive your first reader copies of your new novel. Whatever you do, get creative and show your personality. People on the Internet love videos and they are the most shared media across all social media channels.

Instagram Tip #4: Follow Other Authors

Use the search tool on Instagram to find and follow fellow authors. Try to find authors who have a large following, especially in your genre, and watch their posts to learn how they are using Instagram.

●○○○○ Verizon 📶   1:44 PM   🌙 🔋

🔍 authors ✕   Cancel

TOP   **PEOPLE**   **TAGS**   **PLACES**

authorsimonlaw
Simon David Law • Followed by bookc...

authorskyecallahan
Skye Callahan

writers__corner
👑Aspiring∞Authors👑 • Followed by b...

authorsuzanneyoung
Suzanne Young

author_slw
Slw

authorshelman
Author Eric A. Shelman

authorsloanj
Sloan Johnson • Followed by bookcov...

A sampling of authors from a search on Instagram.

Instagram Tip #5: Share Cover Reveal

When you are ready to reveal your new book cover to the world, Instagram is a great place to post the graphic. Make sure you include a link to a pre-order page or to your author website when you do along with the appropriate hashtags.

You can also hold a book cover vote by creating a diptych (side by side) photo of two design choices. Ask you followers to vote on which cover they like the best.

Instagram Tip #6: Post Quotes

Yes, Instagrammers love quotes too. Use Quozio (mentioned previously under Pinterest) to create visual and interesting quotes from your books or a program like Photoshop or GIMP to create a layer of text over one of your own photographs or an image you have the license to use.

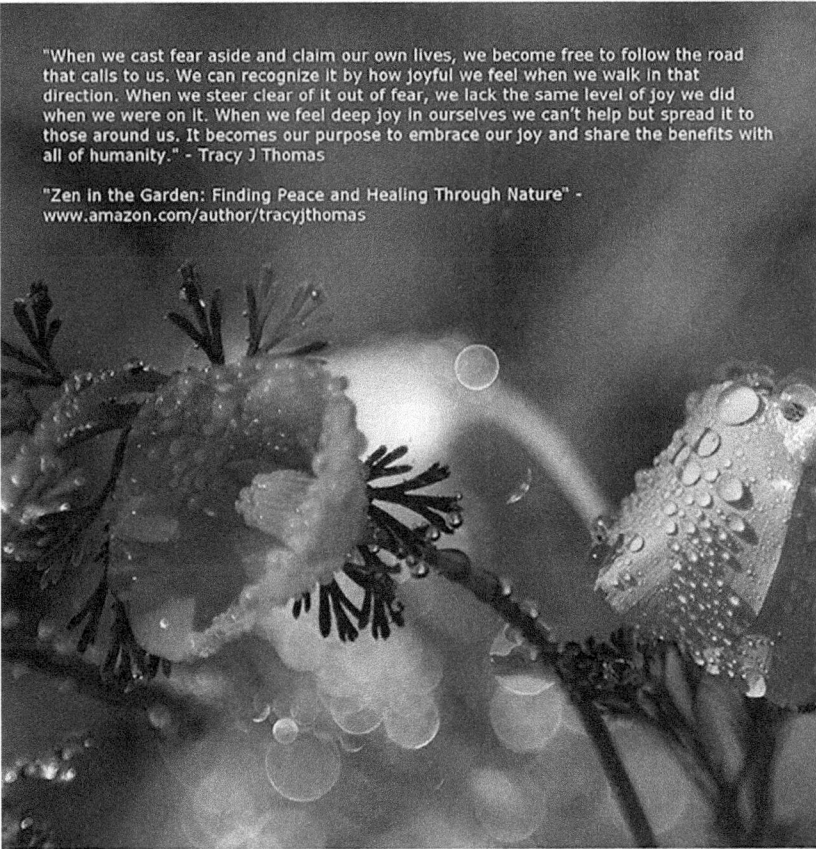

One of my posts on Instagram that shows a quote from my book "Zen in the Garden" layered over one of my photographs that appear in the book.

Instagram Tip #7: Use Hashtags

Similar to other social media spaces, if you want your posts to get noticed, include hashtags.

Some of the best hashtags to use on Instagram to gain like-minded followers are #writersofinstagram (with over 1,009,134 posts), #writers, #writingcommunity, and #writersofig.

Here are several of the best hashtags to use across all social media channels to connect with readers: #GreatReads, #books, #bookworm, and #mustread.

CHAPTER 10. ACTION STEP #7: INCREASE THE NUMBER OF LIKES ON YOUR VIDEOS AND NUMBER OF SUBSCRIBERS TO YOUR YOUTUBE CHANNEL

Other than appearing face-to-face in front of an audience in a physical space, video is the best vehicle for your readers to get to know you as a human being and an author. There is just something about being able to view the face, look into the eyes, hear the intonation of the voice, and to watch the body language of the person who appears on the screen that makes their message that much more compelling and believable.

Another reason to create videos is they provide you with additional content to use across your website, blog, and all social media channels. Videos are the most viewed and shared content across the Internet.

If you don't already have a YouTube channel, then I encourage you to create one. You may not be the most comfortable human being in front of a camera, however, there are creative ways to go about making videos that will definitely drive more traffic to your website or social media accounts and help to spread the word about your writing.

YouTube Tip #1: Create a Book Trailer

Video book trailers are an excellent way to capture the attention of potential readers and to create a certain level of suspense and excitement about your next release. If you have a YouTube channel, people who find and like your book trailer can follow your channel to receive your new video updates.

If you are unclear as to how to create a book trailer, there are many individuals on the Internet who are willing to create one for you. A great and inexpensive place to start is on Fiverr.com. Starting at just $5, there are many Fiverr sellers who will create your next book trailer for you. Make sure you read through their reviews and take a look at their book trailer examples before you make your choice.

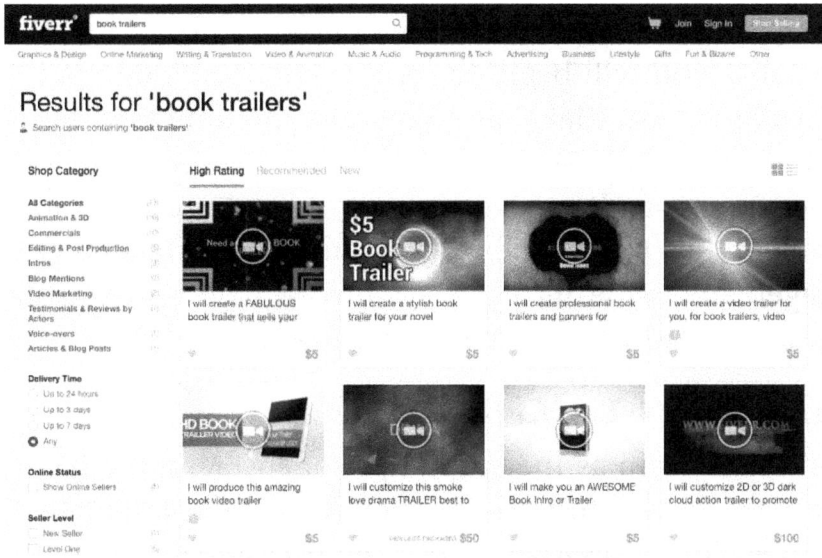

Screenshot of a few results from a search for book trailer creators on Fiverr.

Once you have your exciting new book trailer in hand, post it on your YouTube channel and share it across all your social media accounts and to your website and in a blog post. Remember to use links back to your YouTube channel so people can follow you there.

YouTube Tip #2: Tag Your Videos

When you post a video on your YouTube Channel, make sure you use tags (keywords) so people can find your videos when they do an Internet or YouTube search. Make sure you include your book title, your author name, the book's genre, book's subject, or other relevant terms that have to do with your book or you as an author as your tags.

YouTube Tip #3: Respond to Comments

Inevitably you will begin to receive comments on your YouTube videos. Make sure you take the time to check your channel daily and spend some time responding to those comments. When you make a point to respond to comments it falls in line with the basic tenets of engagement while using social media. The more you engage, the more loyal fans you will gain.

YouTube Tip #4: Be Creative

In the same vein as the video tips for Instagram, when you make videos to post to your YouTube channel, be creative. Yes, it is great to post the occasional video of book signings or a video of your book launch and reading at the local bookstore, but it is better to create videos that have to do with the human being behind the writing. Create videos that speak to your creative process, your inspirations, or even a random question and answer session on the streets with strangers asking them questions about topics you cover in your books would make compelling material. Creativity, authenticity, humor, and a dose of reality are what sell when it comes to video on social media.

To get ideas on how other authors use YouTube, do a search on Google for "list of top YouTube channels by authors" and you will be provided with a long list of links to explore.

Goodreads Listopia has a great list titled "Books by YouTubers: Books written by YouTubers or books written by authors with active YouTube accounts. This would be a great place to start for inspiration.

Listopia

Books By YouTubers

Books written by YouTubers, or books written by authors with active YouTube channels

All Votes   Add Books To This List

1   **A Work in Progress**
by Connor Franta
★★★★½ 4.50 avg rating — 7,490 ratings
score: 9,413, and 96 people voted
Want to Read | Rate this book ★★★★★

2   **The Fault in Our Stars**
by John Green (Goodreads Author)
★★★★½ 4.33 avg rating — 1,798,723 ratings
score: 8,748, and 89 people voted
Want to Read | Rate this book ★★★★★

3   **The Amazing Book is Not on Fire**
by Dan Howell
★★★★½ 4.59 avg rating — 6,640 ratings
score: 8,725, and 89 people voted
Want to Read | Rate this book ★★★★★

4   **Girl Online (Girl Online, #1)**
by Zoe Sugg
★★★★ 3.80 avg rating — 22,621 ratings
score: 6,742, and 69 people voted
Want to Read | Rate this book ★★★★★

5   **Paper Towns**
by John Green (Goodreads Author)
★★★★ 3.95 avg rating — 541,053 ratings
score: 6,702, and 69 people voted
Want to Read | Rate this book ★★★★★

6   **Binge**
by Tyler Oakley (Goodreads Author)
★★★★½ 4.46 avg rating — 7,049 ratings
score: 6,373, and 66 people voted
Want to Read | Rate this book ★★★★★

7   **Username: Evie**
by Joe Sugg
★★★★ 4.14 avg rating — 1,737 ratings
score: 4,959, and 52 people voted
Want to Read | Rate this book ★★★★★

A screenshot from the Goodreads Listopia list "Books by YouTubers."

YouTube Tip #5: Shadow Other Authors

Not only should you search out and follow other authors' YouTube channels, you should also shadow authors who have a strong following on YouTube. Study what they post, read the comments, make comments to their posts, like, and share their videos. Emulate their successes by trying to create something similar, catered for your subject matter and your personality.

In October of 2015, three books written by successful YouTube personalities Tyler Oakley, PewDiePie, and the duo of Dan Howell and Phil Lester, made it into the top 20 on Publisher's Weekly overall best sellers list. These particular YouTube dynamos were not authors first. Their focus was instead on building an audience as dynamic YouTube personalities. The books came later. However, since they had such a large built-in audience, the moment they released their books, the sales were astronomically high.

Their success is a case study for building a strong author platform before you release your books. All the more reason to get your self on YouTube and at least begin to study what these top authors and YouTube personalities are doing that is bringing them a tremendous amount of followers and success.

YouTube Tip #6: Link Your Social Media to Your YouTube Channel
Like all of your other social media, websites, and blogs, remember to link your social media accounts to your YouTube channel. It's all about making it easy for your fans to follow you elsewhere.

CHAPTER 11. ACTION STEP #8: INCREASE THE AMOUNT OF TIMES YOUR POSTS GET STUMBLED ON STUMBLEUPON

There is a whole sub-section of social media tools meant specifically for discovering, sharing and bookmarking posts that has the potential to drive a large amount of traffic to your website or blog. One of them is StumbleUpon.

Users of StumbleUpon basically bookmark (share) links to content or posts they discover on a variety of subjects across the Internet. Other users of StumbleUpon find these links and stumble them into their own lists. When your posts get stumbled, they have the potential of going viral which will in turn drive a ton of traffic to your website or blog.

StumbleUpon Tip #1: Find, Share & Comment on Blogs

When you do a search for blog posts on StumbleUpon, then stumble (share) and comment on those posts, you are bound to have your own posts stumbled (shared) in return just like on any other social media site.

StumbleUpon tip #2: Stumble Your Own Blog Posts

You can stumble virtually any content you find on the Internet to your StumbledUpon account. Make sure you also stumble your own blog posts on occasion so they can be discovered and shared in turn.

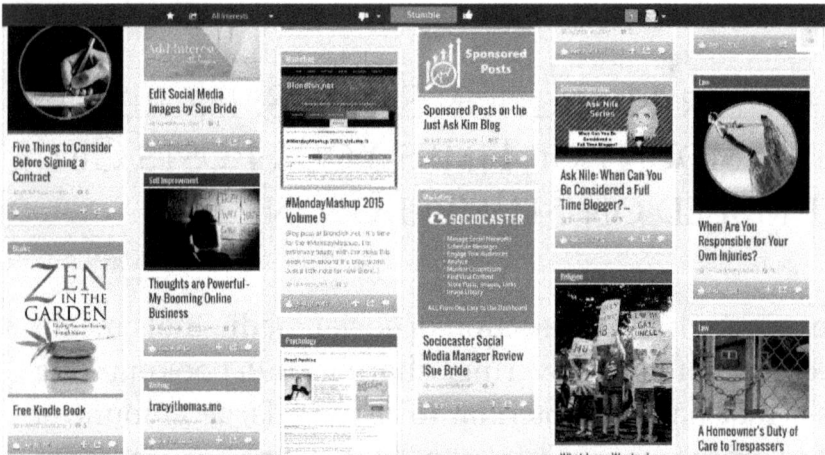

Some of the pages I have stumbled, including my own blog posts. Quite a bit of traffic to my blog originates from StumbleUpon.

StumbleUpon Tip #3: Use Paid Discovery

The StumbleUpon Paid Discovery option provides StumbleUpon users with the opportunity to create affordable ad campaigns based on your specified user budget. When users list an interest in a specific topic that your website or blog addresses, the direct link to your site will be presented to these users. The program does not use banners or text links; instead users are served a direct link to your page.

To find out more about StumbleUpon's Paid Discovery, visit www.ads.stumbleupon.com.

Check out StumbleUpon in order to download the app at www.stumbleupon.com.

Chapter 12. Action Step #9: Build Your Audience on Periscope With Live Broadcasts

The Periscope app is an exciting smartphone app that provides users with the ability to create live-streaming video broadcasts across the Internet.

Owned by Twitter, Periscope gives users the option for your "scopes" (videos) to be watched by your built-in Twitter followers, but also by others across the Web who don't already follow you.

Viewers have the ability to interact with you during a "scoping" (broadcast) through live messaging that appears on your screen. They can also send you heart emojis by tapping on their smartphone screen during your scope. You can interact with your viewers by verbally acknowledging their messages or questions.

Your broadcast can be replayed for up to 24 hours after the event and you can set the app to save your videos to your smartphone if you choose for later use.

With over 10 million users and climbing, I cannot emphasize enough how exciting the possibilities are for its use.

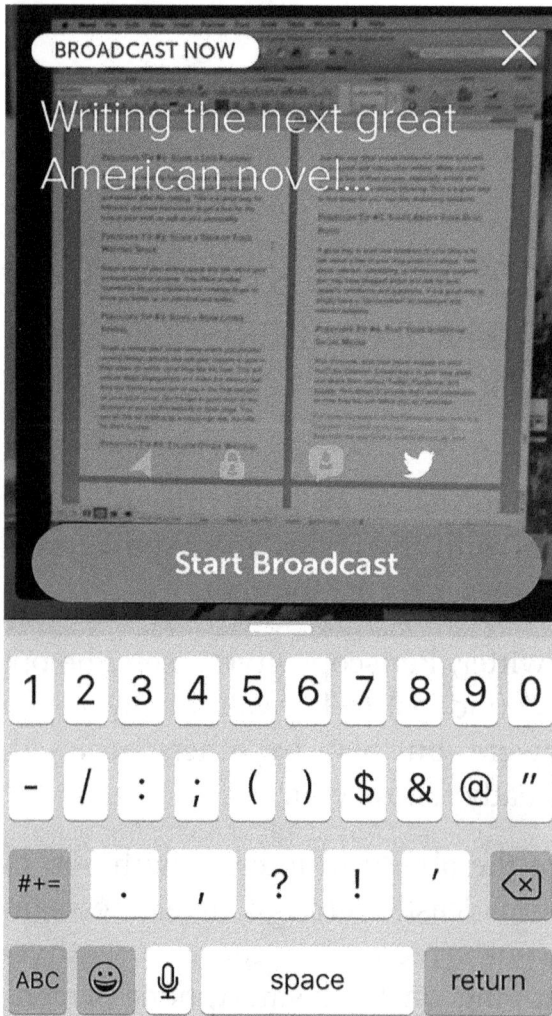

This screenshot is an example of a scope (broadcast) you could

do that talks about your writing process and provides your viewers with a peek into your next book.

Periscope Tip #1: Scope a Live Reading

Scope a live reading from a chapter in your book or a work in progress. Then open it up for live question and answer after the reading. This is a great way for followers and new discoverers to get a feel for the tone of your work as well as your personality.

Periscope Tip #2: Scope a Tour of Your Writing Space

Scope a tour of your writing space and talk about your personal creative process. This offers another opportunity for your followers and newbies to get to know you better as an individual and author.

Periscope Tip #3: Scope a Book Cover Reveal

Scope a reveal of your book cover where you present several design options and ask your viewers to type in their votes on which cover they like the best. This will ensure direct engagement and help the viewers feel they are having some sort of say in the final decision on your book cover.

Don't forget to point them in the direction of your author website or book page. You can do this by holding up a visual sign with the URL for them to copy or make an announcement of where they can find it.

To build excitement around your book cover reveal broadcast, make sure you mention the day and time several days in advance on all your social media channels so your followers will know about it and spread the word.

The broadcast will be a great way to garner new viewers and potential readers as long as you link your Twitter account to the broadcast. You can do this by clicking on the Twitter icon on your broadcast screen prior to the start of your broadcast.

Periscope Tip #4: Follow Other Writers

Just like any other social media tool, make sure you do a search and follow other writers who use Periscope. Make a point to watch a few of their scopes, especially writers who have developed a strong following like Jeff Goins who as of this writing has 5,833 followers and 73,292 hearts (likes) just on Periscope alone. This is a great way to discover ideas for your own live streaming sessions.

When you join in on other writer's scopes, make sure you comment, ask questions, and send hearts!

Periscope Tip #5: Scope About Your Blog Posts
A good way to lead new followers on Persicope to your blog is to talk about a few of your blog posts in a scope. Talk about relevant, interesting, or controversial subjects you may have blogged about recently (or intend to blog about) and ask for your viewer's comments and questions. It is a great way to simply have a "conversation" on important and relevant subjects. At the end of your broadcast, encourage your viewers to pop onto your blog to continue the conversation in the comments section of a specific blog post.

Periscope Tip #6: Post Your Scopes on Social Media
And of course, post your saved scopes on your YouTube Channel, embed them in your blog posts and share them across Twitter, Facebook, and Tumblr. Remember to provide them with information on how they too can follow you on Periscope.

For more information on the Periscope app, you can view this blog post I created about the app: *Favorite Mobile Photo Apps: Periscope by Twitter*. You can view it here: tracyjthomas.me/2015/04/02/favorite-mobile-photo-apps-periscope-by-twitter/. To download the app on your mobile phone, go here: Periscope.tv.

Chapter 13. Action Step #10: Build Your Following as a Goodreads Author

Last, but definitely not least, every author should have an author page on Goodreads. Why? Readers of books of all genres frequent the site, with over 20 million of them to be exact. The opportunity to build your following on Goodreads and to introduce readers to your books is endless.

In addition to readers, Goodreads is an excellent platform to connect with other authors. Following other authors, commenting on and reviewing their books is a great way to draw attention to your own work and gain followers, readers, and reviews in return.

Goodreads Tip #1: Add Your Books to Listopia
Listopia is a section on Goodreads that has listings of books in every category imaginable. Readers peruse

these lists, create their own lists, and vote on individual books within these lists.

Listopia > **Nonfiction Book Lists**

Best Memoir / Biography / Autobiography
3,222 books — 3,647 voters

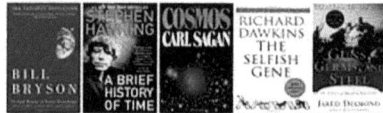

Best Science Books - Non-Fiction Only
958 books — 2,389 voters

Biography and Memoirs that are BETTER than Fiction
1,318 books — 1,858 voters

Best Feminist Books
1,307 books — 1,781 voters

Best Biographies
713 books — 1,696 voters

Must Read Non-Fiction
1,516 books — 1,677 voters

Best American History Books
1,228 books — 1,619 voters

Microhistory: Social Histories of Just One Thing
1,049 books — 1,594 voters

Best Survival Stories
704 books — 1,314 voters

Motivational and Self-Improvement Books
1,017 books — 1,272 voters — you voted for 1 book

This is a screenshot from a few of the Nonfiction Book Lists that appear in Listopia on Goodreads.

Make sure you add all of your books to every appropriate list you can find under Explore/Listopia and watch your books rise towards the top over time asreaders vote for them by giving them a certain amount of stars.

The lists are a great way for readers to discover books and authors they have never before read.

Goodreads Tip #2: Create Book Giveaways

It may seem counter-intuitive, but more often than not, book giveaways result in the sale of more books. Goodreads offers a great book giveaway program that all authors should take advantage of.

You can giveaway as many books as you would like at any given time and schedule the length of the giveaway to last as long as you prefer.

The simple act of having your book appear in the list of books in the giveaway section serves to draw attention to your books and your author page. Viewers can read more about your book and click on the link to view and follow your page. Once the giveaway is over and the winners receive your books, they are encouraged but not required to place a review on Goodreads.

Every time I have run my own giveaway on Goodreads, my sales spike for both Kindle and softcovers during and immediately following the giveaway, more than making up for the cost of the "free" books. I also receive more followers and friend requests on Goodreads as a result.

goodreads   Title / Author / ISBN   Home   My Books   Groups   Recommendations

Giveaways » young-adult

Be the first to read new books! Prerelease books are listed for giveaway by publishers and authors, and members can enter to win. Winners are picked randomly at the end of the giveaway.

Ending Soon   Most Requested   Popular Authors   Recently Listed

The 5th Wave (The 5th Wave, #1)
by Rick Yancey
Release date: May 07, 2013
Enter to win The 5th Wave books signed by the author! The 5th Wave film adaptation is coming to theaters on January 22, 2016.
View Details »

Enter Giveaway

Giveaway ends in:
9 days and 7:10:14

Availability:
5 copies available, 10692 people requesting

Giveaway dates:
Dec 28 - Jan 24, 2016

Countries available:
US

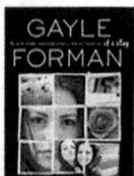

Glass Sword (Red Queen, #2)
by Victoria Aveyard (Goodreads Author)
Release date: Jan 20, 2016
Enter to win a copy of GLASS SWORD, the electrifying sequel to #1 New York Times bestseller RED QUEEN by Victoria Aveyard.
View Details »

Enter Giveaway

Giveaway ends in:
7 days and 7:10:13

Availability:
5 copies available, 9491 people requesting

Giveaway dates:
Dec 14 - Jan 22, 2016

Countries available:
US

I Was Here
by Gayle Forman (Goodreads Author)
Release date: Jan 26, 2016
Enter for a chance to win 1 of 15 paperback copies of I WAS HERE!
View Details »

Enter Giveaway

Giveaway ends in:
11 days and 7:10:14

Availability:
15 copies available, 7081 people requesting

Above is a screenshot of three of the most requested books in the young-adult genre of the book giveaways. The top book listed has 10,692 entries for a chance at one of five signed books.

That is 10,692 sets of eyes that have focused on Rick Yancey's book in the hopes of winning a copy. If they weren't before, all those people who entered are now aware of his book and the majority of them have most likely added it to their Goodreads reading lists.

Now how can you pass up an opportunity like that?

Goodreads Tip #3: Hold Book Discussions

Goodreads allows authors to create featured author groups where authors can hold a question and answer discussion and interact with their readers. It is an excellent way to create buzz surrounding your books and to garner more followers who are interested in your subject and genre.

Goodreads Tip #4: Connect Your Blog

As a Goodreads author, you can integrate your blog posts into your Goodreads author page. When you do this, your blog posts will appear on your author page and Goodreads will email your followers to let them know you have posted a new blog post. This is a wonderful way to drive new traffic to your blog.

* Note: these are all the books on Goodreads for this author. To add more, click here.

TRACY J. THOMAS'S BLOG · 30 posts

Thanks – You Are Steller!

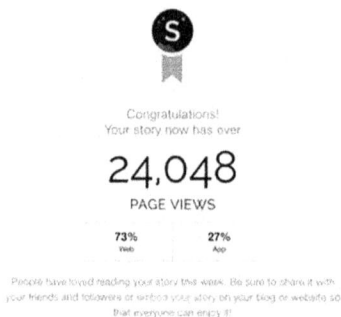

Congratulations!
Your story now has over

24,048
PAGE VIEWS

73% Web · 27% App

People have loved reading your story this week. Be sure to share it with your friends and followers or embed your story on your blog or website so that everyone can enjoy it!

Published on January 07, 2016 15:45

Just a quick post to say thank you all for your support for my recent post about my favorite mobile storytelling app Steller. My Steller story "Pow Wow" has received over 24k page views and yesterday it reached the #2 position of Most Viewed on Steller.

Now let's see if it's possible to double that!
https://steller.co/s/5EeDxX32fH6

If you have already had the chance to view "Pow Wow," here is a l...

View more on Tracy J. Thomas's website »

Read more of this blog post »

Like · 0 comments · flag

View all 30 posts »

My most recent blog post integrated automatically into my Goodreads author profile leading to more blog followers, likes, and shares.

CHAPTER 14. BONUS TIPS

Bonus Tip #1: Skype and Facetime

Contact book clubs around the country, encourage them to buy and read your book, then offer to Skype or Facetime into their book club meeting to field questions and have a discussion about your work. Make sure to provide the book club facilitator with all of your pertinent links to social media and your author pages.

www.skype.com/en/features/

Bonus Tip #2: Use Steller to Create Visual Stories

Steller is a relatively new visual storytelling app for smartphones that allows users to create compelling stories using photographs, graphic elements, video, and text.

Although most people might think of this type of app as being focused on photographers only, brands are also utilizing the app to create compelling stories that introduce viewers to their products in an inviting manner.

This app seems the perfect fit for writers, since writers are storytellers at heart.

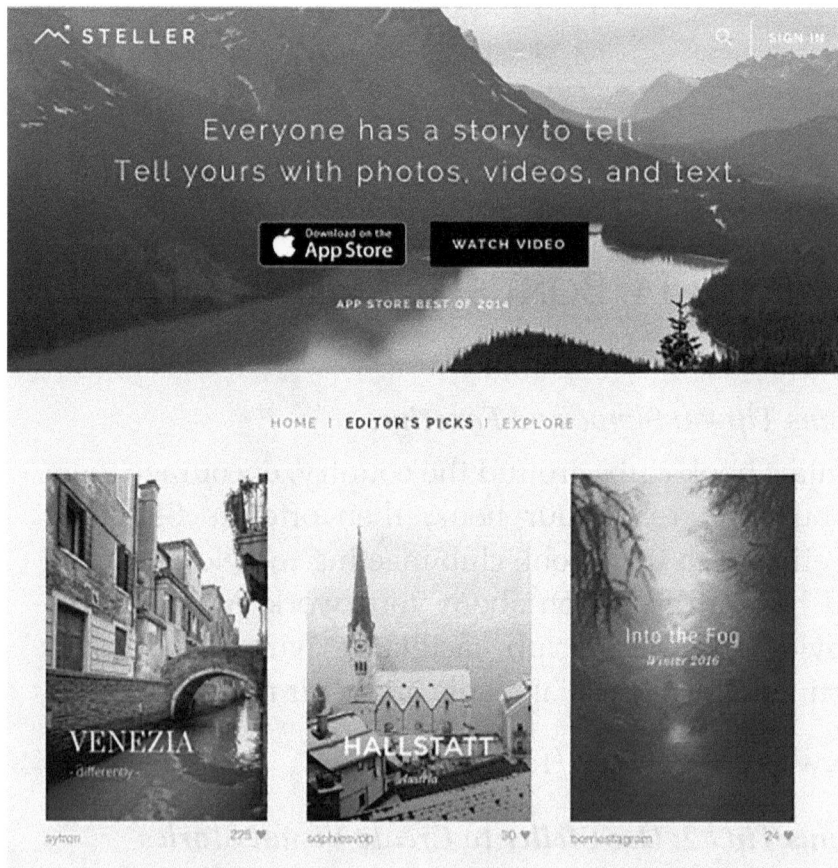

Screenshot from the Steller app website.

You can download the app for free here: steller.co.

For more information on the app, you can read my app review titled *Favorite Mobile Photo Apps – Steller* on my blog at this link: tracyjthomas.me/2016/01/04/favorite-mobile-photo-apps-steller/

For additional bonus tips and information on my other books and guides sign up for my free newsletter here:

DominatingSocialMedia4Authors.com

Bonus Tip #3: Comment on Forums

Forums are a great way to find new followers and readers. Make sure you join forums that pertain to your subject matter or interests and participate by adding to the conversation. Don't use forums as a place for constant sales pitches. If you do you will most likely be blacklisted.

Focus on forums as a place for you to engage with potential followers and readers in an authentic voice. Make sure you include occasional links back to articles or blog posts you have written on specific subject if you feel they are relevant to the conversation and that they will be of assistance to those in that particular discussion.

If you Google "forums for writers" or "forums for people interested in xx," you will be presented with a long list of forum options to explore.

Bonus Tip #4: Create a Flipboard Magazine

Flipboard is a mobile app for both smartphones and tablets that allows users to "flip" through social network feeds of information presented in magazine format.

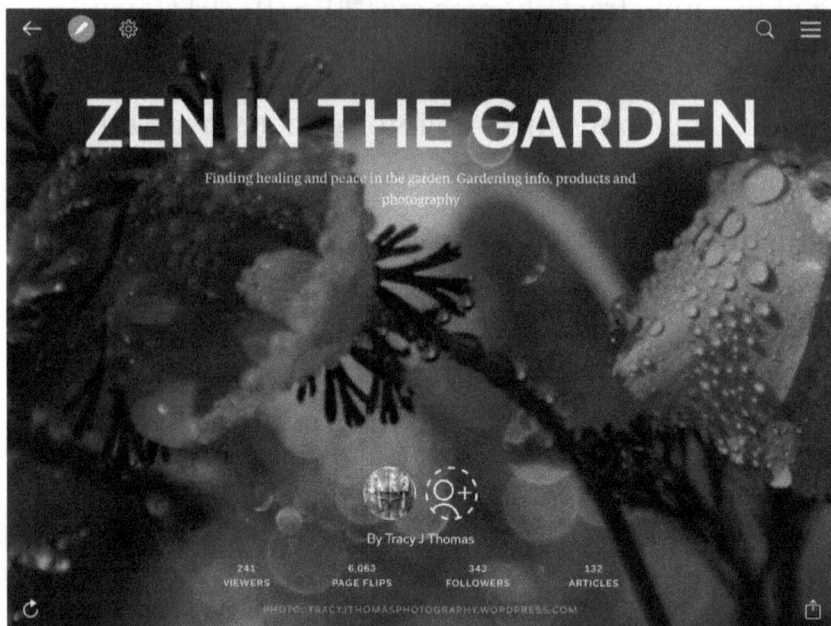

This is a screenshot of the cover of my "Zen in the Garden" magazine on Flipboard.

Flipboard is a great place to find content to share on your own social media accounts like Twitter and Facebook. The best part of Flipboard is you can create your own online magazines filled content that you find on the app and "flip" into your magazines.

Creating your own online Flipboard magazine provides you with a place to share content relevant to your writing or interests. It is also a great place to "flip" your blog post links.

Bonus Tip #5: Give a Workshop or Teach a Class
Workshops and classes are an excellent way to share your knowledge with others and to find new followers. Make a list of all the possible things that fall into your

area of expertise and that you feel you could teach others, especially if those

things relate in some way to the book(s) you are writing or have written.

Do a Google search for writer's conferences or conferences that focus on your area of expertise and look for a call for workshop or class proposals.

Contact your local Parks & Recreation department in your town or city and inquire about teaching courses to the community. Most cities provide opportunities to teach courses to community members and some even pay you to do so.

If your expertise is in the arts, contact your local arts council and inquire if they need any workshop instructors.

Putting your face and personality out there in front of a live audience and people who are interested in your chosen subject matter or genre, is one of the best ways to garner loyal followers.

Bonus Tip #6: Start an Email List

One of the biggest mistakes self-published authors make is failing to create an email list of their readers and followers. The best way to ensure your readers know about any new books, classes, or other product you may put out in the future is to email them the information. The best way to go about this is to create an opt-in form where they can enter their email address with the understanding they will receive something from you in return.

There are a variety of email marketing services that will allow you to create email lists, newsletters, email marketing campaigns, as well as track the results. The service I personally recommend is MailChimp. The service is free for up to 2,000 list members. After you hit the 2,000 mark, the cost varies but is still very affordable.

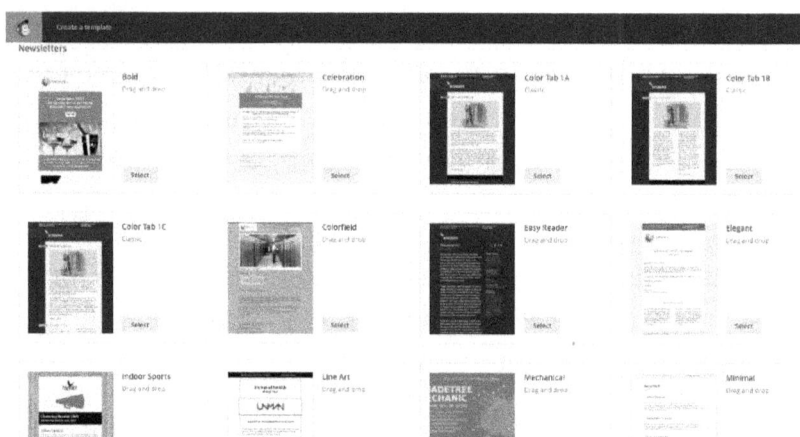

A sampling of a few of the many templates available for free on MailChimp used to create newsletters and email campaigns.

One of the best ways to implement MailChimp is to place a link inside your books, on your blog, your website or on social media. Your link will lead out to a landing page that has a sign up form for whatever item of value you are offering them in return. Whether it is for a newsletter subscription, an excerpt from your next novel, or a free copy of a mini novella, it provides you with a way to capture their email to a specific list for your future marketing efforts.

There are a whole lot of do's and don'ts when it comes to using email lists. One of them is to avoid spamming your list with unnecessary and unwanted sales pitches.

For more information on how to set up and use email lists, **DominatingSocialMedia4Writers.com**.

CHAPTER 15. CONCLUSION

In this book I have presented you with 10 action steps to follow that will assist you in building your author platform. Beneath each action step are several tips to help you reach each goal.

While the amount of information in this short book can feel a bit overwhelming, I encourage you to choose one action and one tip to follow each day, or even one action and one tip each week and just do it. This especially holds true if you are new to the world of social media marketing and are in the process of adapting to the tools.

The most important thing to remember is every little step you take towards building your platform helps, as long as you are consistent in taking those steps.

You will never grow your platform by sitting back and expecting it to happen organically without effort on your part.

Social media is about engagement and involvement. You can't build relationships with all take and no give.

The tools I focused on in this book are far from a complete list of all the social media tools available to authors. However, the tools I presented here have been proven and viable tools for many authors who have successfully built a strong platform.

My hope is that you will approach the task of building your platform with an attitude of excitement, curiosity, and creativity. Think first of all the possible outcomes for your career as a writer if you commit to using these tools right now. Each tool has the potential to place your work in front of literally thousands of new readers. Weave them all together and the potential numbers are staggering.

Please remember this. I am here for the ride right alongside you. I too am continuing to utilize the action steps and tips in my book every day in order to continue to build my own platform.

I am continually testing the waters of the Web to find new and exciting social media marketing options. There are new apps, software, and platforms released on a daily basis. I view it as my job to explore these new offerings and to report back to you on whether or not I believe them to be valuable additions for your marketing arsenal.

You can keep abreast of all the new jewels I find by subscribing to my free newsletter here:

DominatingSocialMedia4Writers.com.

I believe the age of the Internet is one of the most exciting times in which to be alive. Through it, we each have the opportunity to get our work out there in front of the masses

like never before. We also have the opportunity to make connections and to build relationships with people we had a slim chance of meeting in the days before the Web.

We have been handed the opportunity to take control of our brands and to play an integral role in our journey towards success like never before. It is our responsibility as individuals to take the steps to make our dreams become a reality.

So go on now. Get out there and have fun with it!

Appendix: Various Links

Facebook – www.facebook.com
Twitter – www.twitter.com
LinkedIn – www.linkedin.com
Tumblr – www.tumblr.com
Wordpress – www.wordpress.com
Pinterest – www.pinterest.com
Instagram – www.instagram.com
YouTube – www.youtube.com
StumbleUpon – www.stumbleupon.com
Periscope – www.periscope.tv
Goodreads – www.goodreads.com
Steller – www.steller.co
MailChimp – www.mailchimp.com
Flipboard – www.flipboard.com
Skype – www.skype.com

ABOUT THE AUTHOR

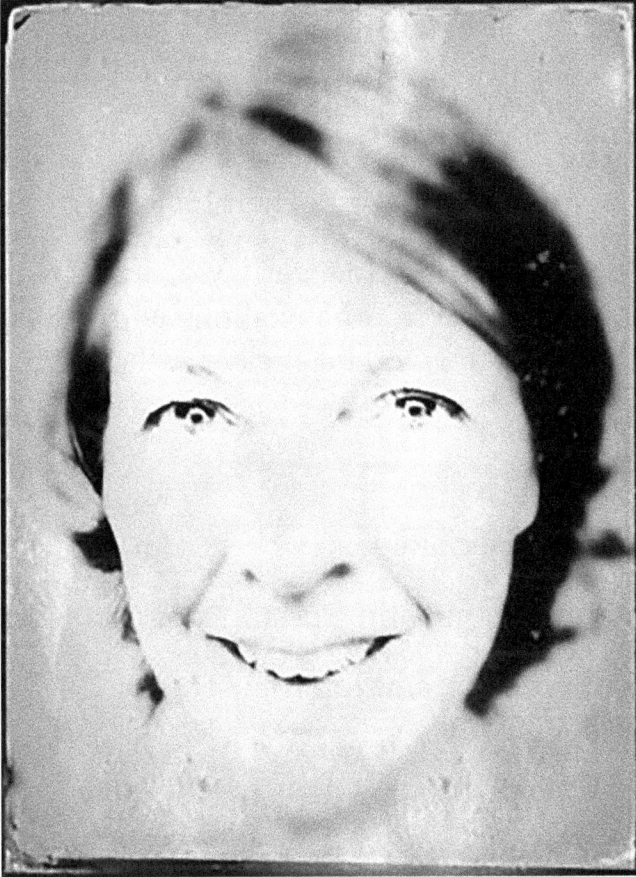

Tracy J Thomas is an award-winning photographer, published author, instructor, website designer, marketing consultant, social media cheerleader, jewelry designer, and nature lover. Very Zen in personality and at heart, she loves helping others envision and create their own success.

She received her M.A. from the University of San

Francisco and her M.F.A. from the Academy of Art University in San Francisco. She is a perpetual student of life and believes we all have important things to teach each other.

Tracy served on staff at the San Miguel International Writers Festival in San Miguel de Allende, Mexico in 2013 where she taught a workshop on social media marketing for writers and was a member of the speaker's panel "Women Write Their Lives."

She has taught workshops to a variety of artists, writers, businesses, and nonprofit organizations with a focus on social media marketing and business development.

Follow or Contact Tracy:

Email Tracy:
tracy@dominatingsocialmedia4writers.com

Free Newsletter: DominatingSocialMedia4Writers.com

Amazon Author Page: amazon.com/Tracy-J-Thomas/e/B00TOYLRVY

Website: www.tracyjthomas.net

Blog: www.tracyjthomas.me

Twitter: www.twitter.com/tjthomasphoto

Instagram: www.instagram.com/TracyJThomas

Facebook:
www.facebook.com/socialmediaforwritersSMA

OTHER BOOKS BY TRACY J THOMAS

On Amazon:

Zen in the Garden: Finding Peace and Healing Through Nature. Big Moose Press. (February 14, 2015). ISBN: 978-0692380574

Dancing at the Shame Prom: Sharing the Stories That Kept Us Small. Seal Press. (September 11, 2012). ISBN: 978-1580054164

Forthcoming:

Walking on the Edge of Crazy: Navigating a Life With PTSD. Big Moose Press. (2016). ISBN: 978-0692456934

One Last Thing...

If you enjoyed this book or found it useful I'd be very grateful if you'd post a short review on Amazon. Your support really does make a difference and I read all the reviews personally so I can get your feedback and make this book even better.

Thanks again for your support!

www.ingramcontent.com/pod-product-compliance
Lightning Source LLC
Chambersburg PA
CBHW070939210326
41520CB00021B/6964